HEROIN

HEROIN

A True Story of Drug Addiction, Hope and Triumph

JULIE O'TOOLE

PUBLISHED BY MAVERICK HOUSE PUBLISHERS

Maverick House, Office 19, Dunboyne Business Park,
Dunboyne, Co. Meath, Ireland.
Maverick House Publishers Asia,
Level 43, United Centre, 323 Silom Road,
Bangrak, Bangkok 10500, Thailand.

info@maverickhouse.com
http://www.maverickhouse.com

ISBN 978-1-905379-53-8

First published in 2005. This edition published in 2008.

DEDICATION

I would like to dedicate this book to my mother for all her love and support, and to my late Da who passed away and whom I love and miss very much. This book is also dedicated to the thousands of drug addicts all over Ireland who think there is no hope for them, and who think they are always going to be drug addicts. Even when things seem desperate, there is always hope.

There is a saying in the world — once a junkie, always a junkie — but my life and this book prove differently.

Acknowledgements

There are so many people I want to thank as there are many people who have helped me get to where I am today. I just want to say 'thank you' to them. They know who they are.

I would like to start with thanking God for giving me a second chance at life, because I know there were many times I should have died, and His hand was on me.

I would also like to thank Pastor Sonny and Julie Arguinzoni for their faithfulness in reaching drug addicts all over the world, as well as my own Pastors Andy and Marie Valdez who I love very much. I also want to thank Victory Outreach Dublin.

A big thanks to Jean Harrington for helping me to write this book and for meeting with me.

My family — Debbie, Olivia, Anthony, Gary, Lindsay, Lee and Ryan who I love very much and who never gave up on me when everybody else did. Thank you to my Ma, who is the best mother in the world. I have never met a woman like her, she has so much love to give and she was always there for me when I was a drug addict, as she is still there for me now. You're the best, Ma!

Thank you to my husband Gerard who I love with all my heart. He is my best friend.

Thank you all.

CHAPTER 1

IF ANYONE HAD told me when I was a child that I would end up a heroin addict, I would have laughed at them. You see, sport was my thrill. Football was how I got a rush. I was one of the best footballers in my area — better than all of the girls except for my sister Olivia, and certainly better than most of the blokes. Olivia and I would race home after school to change into our track suits so we could go down to the playground. I was always in goal and Olivia would lash the balls at me as fast as bullets. She was definitely the best footballer in the area, and we played football every single day as children. She's now an international player on the Irish team.

I come from a working-class background, but I didn't have a bad start in life. I had a structured childhood with set times for everything. I sometimes look back and wonder why I've led the life I have. I have to be honest and say I don't have many answers for you. I don't know where I lost myself but I know I did. I still wonder about the decisions I made, or if they were decisions at all. Was I even given choices about my life? I'm still trying to figure that one out but I know one thing for sure. When I was young I never said to myself, 'I want to be a drug addict when I grow up.'

Heroin wasn't something that I planned to do. The drug was something that crossed my path. I never went looking for it and I don't believe it came looking for me. My drug addiction was something that just happened. You have probably heard people say they were in the wrong place at the wrong time. I think I was one of those people.

I grew up in the heart of Dublin's north inner city. My family lived on Sheriff Street. Most people have heard about Sheriff Street at some point in their lives. It has an awful reputation. When most people think about it, they think about drugs and criminals. They conjure up images of young boys joy riding and stealing. It is true to say that some of the people who have lived there had truly awful reputations. Some of them deserved them but some didn't. I have met most of the major gangsters from the area at some point but I didn't see them as criminals. They were just men from the community. I wouldn't give them a second thought.

The street itself runs from the side of Connolly Station all the way down to the docks. There are several roads leading off it where Dublin Corporation built flat complexes in the 1940s and 1950s. When people say they come from Sheriff Street, they probably mean one of the flat complexes or small council estates that lead off it.

These were the areas that succumbed to heroin, and they have never really recovered from it. Heroin arrived in Dublin in the early 1980s, and it's been around ever since. I was only a child back then but I remember our community changing, though I wasn't sure how or why at the time.

We didn't always live in Saint Brigid's Gardens. Our first home was on a small road off Sheriff Street called Saint Laurence's Street. There were lanes leading down to the flats, and they were so close that if somebody was making dinner down the road you would smell it. They had little back gardens and people used to throw over tea bags and sugar to each other. It was a very close community around Sheriff Street, and everybody looked after each other. It was all right to go in and say to your neighbour, 'Give us a bit of sugar', or even if they weren't there you could go in, take what you needed, and tell them later. There would never be a problem. It was like that. People trusted each other. In every door there was a key.

In the 1980s they knocked down Saint Laurence's and built part of a community centre we used to call The Tarmac, so we had to move on. I didn't care about moving around; all I cared about was playing football, so when Ma said, 'Get your stuff, we're moving,' I just went. We moved to the Saint Brigid's Gardens flat complex when I was around eight or nine years old.

Saint Brigid's Gardens was one of the toughest parts of Sheriff Street. I can think of few places that had its reputation. The people were hard, the streets were hard and everyone knew everyone else's business. It was real inner city Dublin.

That was the way things were in the flats. I could tell you about my neighbours' cousins and their cousins if I had the time. Many people in the inner city inter-marry amongst friends and neighbours and few ever move far away from the city.

I am more comfortable in the city. Even to this day I love it; the smells, the noises and the skyline. It's my home and it relaxes me.

There could be drug dealers standing outside the front door and kids speeding up and down the road in a stolen car and it still wouldn't bother me. I love the city. I love everything about it. I love the anonymity of the streets; I love blending in with the crowd. I'm a townie.

The Gardens was erected by Dublin Corporation to house the working-class of the city and it quickly became a slum. The flats were dismal, but as children we had great fun living there. A few years after moving in, the corporation started blocking off some of the flats and they became squats. Just when we moved into Saint Brigid's, heroin started becoming available all around us. It was everywhere. It lurked in the background of my childhood.

Although I was vaguely aware of the drugs that surrounded me growing up, I didn't take much notice of them. Saint Brigid's Gardens was a great place to live as far as I was concerned, because we had an area to play football in and a playing ground where everyone had a little pram shed they could kick the ball against.

I never went outside the Gardens, other than to go to school or the community centre. I was never allowed onto Sheriff Street itself anyway. If I was caught there I'd be in trouble. But you know if you tell a kid not to go somewhere, they are going to get curious and they're going to go and see why they aren't allowed there. It wasn't until I hit my teens that I even knew why there was a big deal surrounding Sheriff Street. It was then I realised that our community had a serious drug problem.

Saint Laurence's Mansions was one of the first housing schemes to be hit with heroin. It became known for drug dealing and it never lost that reputation until it was demolished in the 1990s.

People would come from across the city to score heroin in Sheriff Street and many of the dealers lived in the area. They sold every type of drug going. The dealers ripped the soul out of the city. I grew up watching this go on. I couldn't help but notice it, but as a child I was more interested in playing football than watching what the adults were doing, so I never thought about it as something damaging. I thought everyone lived like us.

* * * * *

Some people have the impression that families reared in working-class areas are neglected, or dragged up by their parents. I suppose I did nothing to help change this image by ending up on heroin, but we had quite a strict upbringing when we were young kids. Our home was old-fashioned, my parents were very conservative, and we had routine and order in the house. We didn't have a lot but we had enough to get by. When you are a child, you never think too much about your own home. I certainly never did. I was too busy having fun. I took our life for granted because I knew no different.

Ma made us all sit down to dinner together when we were young. We had to be in bed at certain times, and we had our curfew. Saturdays were our bath days and you had to have a bath whether you wanted to or not. That was great. I loved the structure of home life. I always knew what was about to happen. I loved my large family even though it had its disadvantages.

For example, we all slept in bunk beds, and it got a bit cramped as we got bigger. When I think back on it I wonder how my parents coped. We were everywhere. We did everything together and we went everywhere together. The house was always full of children.

Our flat had three bedrooms. Ma and Da lived in the front room, looking out over the balcony, and our bedrooms were in the back. It was all the girls together and all the boys together.

My parents Mary O'Brien and Patrick O'Toole were working-class people, and like me, they were also real townies. Ma grew up on Mountjoy Square and Da was from the tenements nearby in Summerhill. They met as teenagers and got married after a few years. They were close at first, but things started to go wrong a few years into their marriage.

Da was a drinker; one who went on binges. He mightn't drink at all for a few weeks, then suddenly he'd lapse and go on a big binge. Because he didn't drink everyday, he couldn't recognise the fact that he had a drink problem.

He worked at the boats on the docks for a long time but work dried up and they let him go. He did a coal run for a while after that, but then he stopped working. After that, he done bits and pieces here and there, but nothing was really permanent.

He was a broken man cos he didn't work regularly. He came from a very traditional family set-up where the man was the provider while the woman stayed at home and reared the children. When he couldn't live up to this ideal, and as we got older and less controllable, he turned to the drink more and more.

Drink destroyed Da and my family. He lost his personality when he had drink on him. He wrecked his health and body, and was a different man when he went on the booze. There was no talking to him.

Every few weeks he would promise Ma that he'd stop. He would stay dry for a while but he would always fall off the wagon. He'd go on binges, then get a job on a building site, and then he'd hit the booze again. He got worse as he got older and trouble came into the family.

The last job he had was in the IFSC, doing security. It was a form of escape for him. He'd be there on his own, watching television, drinking a few cans. He was happy then. He died because of drink. He got ulcers and they burst. Despite all the hurt and pain he brought to the family, I miss him terribly; I know we all do.

* * * * *

Ma and Da didn't really have a relationship or a marriage after a while. They just lived together for our sake. They were just two people living together who got along sometimes, but mostly they argued and fought. I think that's the best way of describing their marriage after we started to go astray.

They were so busy trying to rear the seven of us that they left no time for each other.

They came and went but didn't speak or communicate to each other.

When they weren't fighting, they just existed alongside each other. Any love that had once been between them was long gone by the time I was old enough to realise it. I don't know why they didn't separate or leave home. I suppose they didn't because they had nowhere to go, or maybe they stayed together because of us. I don't know the answer to that question. But I know one thing for sure. Although they often weren't able to show it, they both loved us; I just wish they loved each other more.

My parents made sure we had everything. We never went to school without our lunch. We never went without toys or schoolbooks, even though there were seven of us. I was bang smack in the middle of the family, and from an early age, I never felt like I fully belonged to either group. Debbie was the oldest with Olivia and Anthony close behind. You could say we were like slices of bread — one came after the other. There's just a year between all of us. Then there was me, with Gary, Lindsay and Ryan close behind. While I was growing up, the question that forever occupied my mind was who I should play with. Should I go with the oldies or the young ones? We were all close in age, but we were also very close friends.

If I ever had a problem with anyone, Olivia or Debbie would be down like a shot to sort it out for me. They looked after me and the younger ones growing up. We were that sort of family. We were close. If you messed with one, you messed with us all.

My parents always looked after us no matter how bad things were between them. I have to say, though, that Ma did most of the work. When we were living in Saint Laurence's Street there was only two bedrooms, and all the kids were in a single bed. We hadn't got a bed when we were eight and nine months old so she used to put us in a chest of drawers. That's how she survived.

Life gave her a raw deal. You could say it gave the people of the inner city a raw deal. Ma did what she had to do in order to get by. She used to have to go in to her next-door neighbour and ask for a lend of half-a-shilling or half-a-crown to get us beans on toast or something like that. There were times she hadn't got a penny. Da would be out drinking and she had nothing.

When it got to the point that they weren't coping financially any more, she ended up shoplifting. It started off innocently, robbing messages from the shops, some milk and butter. When she realised that she was actually very good at it, she became more brazen and started doing all her 'shopping' in this fashion. She got away with it for a while, but she eventually got nicked, and went to prison several times for it.

It wasn't until I was much older that I discovered she had been one of the best shoplifters in Dublin. It's not something that she is proud of but she was so good, that at one point the security guards used to call her the Weed, because she could sneak in and out without them noticing. Ma doesn't talk about those days now.

She robbed to make ends meet and looked on it as a means to an end. She thought it was the only way, so she did what she felt she had to do to provide for her family and children. She stopped shoplifting a long time ago, and it was only when I got older and wiser that I realised what she was doing.

At Christmas time she'd make a list of what we wanted, and then she would go down the country to do some 'shopping'. She'd come back with our presents; Levi jeans, runners — everything we'd asked for and more. At the time, I didn't know what was going on. At first, I thought she was making a list of what we wanted so she could give it to Santa. After that, I thought she was making the list so she'd know what to buy us herself. It was only when I got older that I realised she wasn't buying these things, and neither was Santa. She was robbing them.

I have clear memories of her going off to Wales to make money from robbing. She would go on a day trip to Holyhead, fleece the place, and come back with thousands of pounds worth of cigarettes and drink. That's how we had everything we needed growing up.

It was inevitable that she would get caught. You can't get away with that type of thing forever. She was in and out of prison throughout my childhood, but Da always took good care of us while she was away. Although he was very fond of a drink, when she wasn't around he stepped in to fill her shoes. It was only when she came back that he allowed himself to fall to pieces and to start binge-drinking again.

He used to say to us, *your Ma is gone away for a while,* but we didn't understand where she was, or why.

He really did his best for us. Sometimes he'd bring us to see her in prison. We'd all walk up from Sheriff Street to go and see her in Mountjoy Prison. Debbie and Olivia would visit her every week but it was too hard for her having all the younger kids there as well. She'd be broken-hearted, so we only went up every now and then.

At the time, physical contact was allowed between prisoners and visitors, so Ma found it very hard to let go of us when it was time to leave. I was too young to understand what was happening and I used to play with the toys they had there to keep the kids busy. I hardly paid any attention to Ma, until it was time to leave. I used to cry then because I didn't want to leave her behind.

I wanted her to come home with us, and I'd realise that I'd hardly spent any time talking to her. After an hour we were all gathered up and told to say goodbye. When we'd get home in the evening, I'd be wondering why Ma hadn't come home with us. Why did she stay behind? I would get upset then and worried about her being on her own, even though she had a lot of friends in there with her.

I can only imagine how she must have felt. I don't believe that any woman would ever want to leave her children. I never stopped worrying about her when she was inside.

That was only natural cos, as a close family, we always worried about each other and looked out for each other. Children have short memories though, and we just continued with our football and our games and it never seemed long before she was home again.

In a strange way, things were peaceful when she was gone, because Da didn't have anyone to fight with. We were too young to be doing anything to really annoy him, but if we did, he was quite good at dishing out discipline.

He always made sure we were clean and were ready for school. We never missed a day of primary school because of him. We could have been dying of the 'flu but he'd still get us up out of bed. They were important things at the time. He tried to keep a structure in our lives, but it probably wasn't enough to keep us together. It would be difficult for any man to raise seven children in inner city Dublin on his own, never mind someone with a drink problem.

Ma was only ever in prison for three months, or perhaps six months at a time. Once she was in Holloway prison after she got caught shoplifting with her friend. She'd be in and out of jail all the time and overall, she spent 10 years behind bars. It was always good having her around, until she got sent away again.

You might ask if I'm embarrassed about this now. I'm not. I'm proud of my Ma. I can see that she's got strength of character. She had to feed her children, and she didn't shirk her responsibility. She did what she had to to survive.

Chapter 2

WHAT HAPPENED IN my family could be seen as an example of what happened in many families, not only in working-class areas, but across the class divide. We started out as a family full of love and hope . . . but life somehow got in the way. My parents were once young, vibrant and full of life and love, but by the time I was old enough to be aware of their relationship, all that was left was resignation and bitterness.

Although they took care of us and loved us, there was a gaping hole in my life growing up. For some reason I didn't feel loved. I didn't feel special. I was the middle kid in a family of seven, and maybe this is the only reason for my insecurities, but I always felt that

Ma and Da were too busy fighting to spend time loving us. I blamed them for this for years, but I've since gone to counselling and I know that they were just victims of their own circumstances.

Ma and Da did their best for us, and I don't blame them for the bad decisions I made in my life. I don't blame them for my ending up on heroin.

I know they loved me, but I did feel at the time that I was raised without the love and affection I needed. Ma and Da had never been shown affection growing up, so they found it hard to show it to us. I'm real affectionate, and I knew affection was missing in my life. As a kid, I always said to myself that when I get married I'm going to love that person and I'm going to make sure that they love me. Hitting somebody and screaming at them is not showing love. From a young age I knew the difference between love and abusing somebody like that.

I saw Da hitting Ma once, and came to know what love was, only because I knew it was missing. As a child growing up, I never knew what it felt like to have someone show you affection and support. When I came home from school, they would just say, 'Do your homework and then you can go out!' And that was it. There was no real interaction; no real communication between us. Ma says, when poverty comes in the door, love goes out the window, and she's right.

I know deep down both Ma and Da loved me, but I just wish they could have shown it more. When you're a child, you need hugs and love and I think I never got enough of that. I think showing love and support is more important than giving someone a €200 mobile phone, or buying them a car, or giving them money. Putting your arms around your child and saying, 'Well done, I'm proud of you,' will stay with them longer than receiving a present.

It's sad really, but the thing is, the best memories for me were all to do with football and the playground — things that happened away from home. I don't even remember getting a hug when I done well at a tournament or anything like that. The only people that really hugged me during my childhood were the girls on the football team after we won. Everyone would jump around going, 'Yay!' hugging each other.

Sometimes Da would hug me when he was drunk. He'd wrap his arms around me and kiss me and rub his beard on me and go, 'I love you, Scoochy-Moochy.' That was my nickname then. I hated the smell of drink off him. It was rotten. He'd never say, 'I love you,' when he was sober. Ma did, but not very often. She'd give me an awkward kind of hug and she'd tell me that I looked lovely. But she found it difficult to be physically affectionate to all of us cos there were so many, and I really missed that growing up.

The distinct lack of love and respect between our parents had a big effect on me. There was often a horrible atmosphere in the house, and that made it hard for me to be around. We'd be sitting at the table and there'd be stupid arguments, over nothing. Ma and Da would suddenly start screaming at each other. I'd be sitting there thinking to myself, 'Ah, here we go again.'

'Ah, Ma, will you stop it? Don't be fighting!' I'd sometimes say, trying to calm her down.

Seeing my parents' arguing with each other like that was terrible. If we opened our mouth to pass any comment we'd get a slap across the head. I often tried to stop them fighting, cos I knew if Ma started fighting with him, he'd go off and get drunk. When he'd come back, the problems would start for real.

Da never done anything bad when he was sober. He wasn't naturally aggressive. It was only when he was drunk that it turned to violence.

* * * * *

I still have the images in my head of him hitting her. The memory never leaves me and I don't think it ever will.

I decided when I was 10 years old that I would never end up like that. I'd rather not live in that kind of atmosphere; because when a mother and father's relationship breaks down like that it damages the kids. They stayed together for our sake, but the truth is, they probably should have separated for our sake.

I was terrified while they were fighting; I was terrified when Da went out drinking for the night, because I knew what would happen when he returned.

The pictures in my head will never leave me, no matter how much counselling I get. If anyone raises their voice around me now, the fear returns in an instant. I revert to the little girl in the flat, wondering if Ma was going to die. Once or twice Da left her really hurt and he wouldn't let us go near her to help her.

Olivia or Debbie would take over when things spun out of control like that. They'd lock us in the bedroom cos they'd be afraid that if we went down, he'd hit us too. My older sisters were real protective of us. The constant aggro and threat of violence that we lived with made us close as children. We were always closest at night time, because we were bundled up in the bed, and we knew what might be coming. We would cower under the blankets when we'd hear the front door slam, and wonder if he'd just fall asleep on the couch or if he'd be looking for a row.

Ma had a couple of barring orders against Da, and loads of times when he'd arrive in an aggressive mood, the guards were called. When the guards arrived, he was generally sitting in a drunken stupor so they'd just handcuff him and take him away. They'd leave him in the station overnight and then he'd come back the next day sober, not knowing what he said, or even what he'd done.

When I was older I asked him, 'How come you don't say any of this when you're sober?' He wouldn't answer me because he couldn't remember. But he hated what he done; he knew what he was doing was wrong, but he couldn't help himself. It wasn't really him doing it I suppose; it was the drink. It was the whiskey that done it to him.

When he knew he was doing wrong he just put his head down. That was probably a horrible feeling, for him to be letting his family down; cos I'm sure he didn't intend to be like that.

I now hate violence of any kind, especially when someone is violent towards another who is weaker and smaller than them. I think Da was more afraid of losing control of us than anything else, and the drink made him braver. When he would sober up he was like, 'Oh I didn't mean it,' but then he'd go out the following night and he'd do the same thing again.

When he was acting up, Ma would just bottle it all up and wouldn't say anything until the next day. She was afraid of him when he was drunk, but when he sobered up the next morning she'd let loose and start roaring at him. Ma would run amok and she'd lunge into him. She would never give out to him when he was drunk because there was no point; he'd never remember.

She'd be on and on at us, saying, 'Tell him what he was saying, tell him.'

We'd be all terrified, so we wouldn't say anything, but she sure would. In the end, he still wouldn't remember.

She'd throw him out, but he never stayed away for long. Things would be quiet until his return. He always came back, eventually. Ma probably felt she had to take him back because he'd die, without a proper place to live. He'd be hanging around with people drinking really cheap drink so it was better that Da was at home, where at least he'd be sober some of the time.

Things would be okay for a short while when he'd first return, because he'd be on his best behaviour, but not for long.

Anything could trigger a row. For example, if Dublin lost a big Gaelic match, I didn't even dare close my eyes after that. We'd be sitting there at night with the blankets over our head going, 'When's Da going to come in, when's he going to come in?'

When he would come home then, full of whiskey, all we would hear is, 'Brian Mullins, Barney Rock, Kevin Moran . . .'

I knew all the players' names cos he'd be talking about them to the wall, and he'd just get so out of control it was scary. The whiskey really turned him.

In between all the fights and all the madness, he still didn't know how to show us that he loved us. Although he knew he had a problem, in those days you didn't know what you were supposed to do about it.

Da was always old-fashioned in the sense that we weren't allowed to bring any boyfriends home. My brothers weren't allowed to bring girlfriends back either, or he'd threaten to chop their hands off. If we were ever brave enough to bring someone home, we weren't allowed to sit beside them or hold hands or he'd completely freak out. With that same old-fashioned view, he assumed he was head of the household, and therefore entitled to a drink.

I'm sure he did know that he had a drinking problem, but I don't think he knew how bad it was; on himself, on Ma, or on us as a family.

The sad thing is that the memories that stay with me the most are when Da started hitting us and throwing digs at us, especially when he started to hit Ma. He got worse and worse with his binge drinking, especially as we were all getting older and starting to lead lives he didn't approve of. He placed great emphasis on order and structure, and when I hit my teens, I rebelled against all that, as did Debbie. Da found it hard to understand why he was losing control of his children, and he reacted with drink and aggression.

* * * * *

I sometimes look back at my childhood and wonder what it was that made me turn to heroin. I'd wonder, 'How did I get myself like that? What was it that drove me to do that?' Sometimes I think it was just that I was in the wrong place at the wrong time . . . but it was my own decision to be at that place at that time, so ultimately I have to take responsibility for my decisions.

I've come to realise that a major problem throughout my life was that I felt like I had no place in life. I was stuck somewhere I wasn't supposed to be, cos I didn't feel loved where I was.

Despite this I was a very happy-go-lucky child. Despite what was happening in the house, I had everything I wanted. I had a great childhood with my brothers and sisters. It was fun-filled and carefree.

But when I'd hear Ma and Da fighting, I always told myself that I'd never be like that; I'd never act like that in front of children, and if I have kids I'll always give them the one thing I didn't get; love and affection.

Christmas is a good example of what my family life was like back then. For us kids it was a mixed blessing. It was always exciting, cos I was getting presents and Santa was coming. Everybody would be on their best behaviour but still, Da would always ruin it.

Christmas wasn't Christmas without him getting buckle drunk and starting a row; that was Christmas all over. I can remember very few Christmases when he didn't do that. He'd get drunk and aggressive, and would just keep drinking until he passed out. And that was it; the end of him. He would be knocked out for the night and wouldn't remember a thing.

CHAPTER 3

YOU MIGHT THINK that my childhood had nothing but violence and fear in it, but that's not true. It *is* a part of my history, that's true, but I had a lot of good times too, especially when I was playing football.

Sport was my thing. We were a real sporting family. All the children played sport and games. When it rained, we'd all go round to the Laurence O'Toole Community Centre, or as we called it, Gals, on Sheriff Street, and play snooker, darts and table tennis. But when the weather was fine, we used to hang out in the local playground. We called it the Alley-O. We'd play five-a-side football there all day, every day after school. We'd just play soccer together, me and my sisters, all day long.

We were soccer mad. I was always in goals and they'd queue to take shots. That is except for Debbie.

She loved tennis, but as she got older she was more into clothes and make-up. I always looked up to Debbie, but I never really got into all of that; I remained a tomboy.

Olivia and I used to enter a team into the Finglas five-a-side tournament, and when we'd win it, we'd be over the moon. This was the best thing that could happen to football crazy kids from the inner city. We'd go on about it for ages because it was a big thing to win the Finglas five-a- side. It was so competitive. We won trophies and tournaments all the time, and this was a great buzz.

People from all over Dublin entered teams into the competition, and most of the times we won it. We were lucky to have Olivia looking after the team though. She'd pick the best players, so we always knew we were going to win. Even though we only won a little scabby trophy, it was like the best thing in the world to us. We'd be carrying it around, bringing it to school and showing it to everybody. It was great. I used to tag along with Olivia all the time cos we were really close.

She used anything she could get her hands on to train with. She'd get bikes, bricks and an assortment of junk, and place them on the ground. I'd be in goal, watching her weave in and out between them, hoping that she wouldn't hit it too hard.

'Don't lash it,' I'd scream at her when she got close to me, but she had such a powerful kick that I'd just get a bang of it. I was very competitive too, and I'd never let her get a goal on purpose, even if it meant I'd go home black and blue from the thumps of the ball.

She'd do that all day after school. She'd bring the football to school and then for her lunch hour all she'd do was play with the ball. She wouldn't even eat; she'd just practise with the ball at every opportunity.

My love of sport is down to her. I loved it then, and I still do. Today I can play any type of sports, just because I used to go to Gals after school.

That was my highlight, going to play sports after school every day. I loved going, cos I was real energetic and I always had loads of friends there. It was an escape from home and I hated going back because I knew what I was going back to.

* * * * *

Sheriff Street was great when I was a kid, before the drugs and drug addicts became more and more common. It had real community spirit and everybody knew and looked out for each other. If someone from another area came in, everyone would be checking them out, and someone would walk up and ask what they were doing on Sheriff Street.

The different flats had their own gangs — Brigid's Gardens, Shanahan's, and Laurence's — so we'd be in competition with each other all the time, trying to be the best gang. It was very lively, but it was all harmless fun. The gangs we were in were innocent and we didn't do anything other than play football and hang around all day long. At Halloween we'd have bonfires and everybody would come out to watch. We all knew each other. There were no strangers there.

I went to Saint Laurence O'Toole's primary school for girls in the North Wall. My brothers went to the Christian Brothers School on Oriel Street. I was never really into school though. I didn't like to study and couldn't have cared less about my homework. The only thing I was interested in at school was art, but I hated everything else. Most of all, I hated having to wear a uniform, cos it meant wearing a skirt. I used to tear it off the minute I got home from school, put on a tracksuit and head down to the Alley-O or Gals.

The only thing I liked about school was the playground. The playground was my life. And I used to go mad at the weekends when it wasn't open. I used to play football tournaments most Saturdays, or we'd go winkle-picking in Sutton or something like that. Someone from the community would take us out. Neighbours looked after each other in those days — it was so close. There was none of this competition about who had the best house, or this fascination with having the best runners, or clothes, or all that either. It wasn't like that.

I used to go to school with odd stockings, and be lucky. I'd think I was blessed if I got a jam sandwich for lunch. Nobody had anything, and everybody was happy with what they had. That's the way I remember it.

We always had a dog growing up. We had a mongrel named Pippi for years and she got so old that she couldn't get up the stairs anymore.

We couldn't carry her, so we used to have to leave her down in the little electricity shed at the bottom of the flats. We were devastated when she died cos she was the longest living dog we ever had. Ma got a little Jack Russell, Buster, after that. Buster used to sleep with us in the bed. We knew he'd be outside and one of us would be like, 'Get the dog, get the dog, it's too cold.' We'd bring him in and he'd be under the blankets. He was part of the family, and a family's not a family without a dog.

* * * * *

Like many other kids from the area, when I started Parnell Secondary School I ended up mitching most of the time. After a few months, I stopped going altogether. Ma soon caught me and grounded me. She wouldn't let me out to play at all. The hardest thing was having to sit in my room all weekend and listen to all the other kids playing football just below me. It didn't make any difference to me though, because come Monday morning I'd just go on the mitch again. I knew Debbie had stopped going to school already, and she was staying home all day, so I didn't see why I should have to go.

Ma then kept me at home, when she realised that I had no intention of going back to Parnell. She said it was better for me to be home than hanging around the streets, and she used to give me housework to do so I'd be busy all day. The house would shine after I cleaned it. After a few weeks of this, she softened a bit and used to let me out to the playground in the afternoon.

Debbie started going to a place called Slot 2 on Sheriff Street. Everyone called it Bosco's because Paul Byrne who used to be on Bosco, the children's programme that was on television in the 1980s, used to run it. It was set up to educate kids who had stopped going to school. Bosco's had a relaxed atmosphere and it was very easy-going, so it was very difficult to rebel against. It housed a collection of unruly and rebellious teenagers from all across the inner city.

After a few months, my parents and the school just stopped trying to get me to go to Parnell Street, and Ma said I could go to Bosco's. I was delighted because loads of my mates were there already. I thought I was real cool for going there. It was the place to be. I felt like I belonged to a certain type of people. It was where all the hard cases and trouble-makers were sent. If you were going to Bosco's, it meant you were getting away with murder; that nobody could tell you what to do.

Classes started at ten o'clock in the morning, but you could do what you wanted — you could smoke, come in at eleven o'clock or whenever. They gave us lunch there as well, so I never went home. They tried to have classes but we just disrupted them all the time. It would always get out of control cos there were a lot of rebellious kids there who had never been to any school and just had no interest.

At first I wanted to do well in school, cos there were other girls who were doing well at it. But because I was a tomboy, I saw them as being too 'girly' and I thought it was a sign of weakness to be in studying when everyone else was out having a laugh.

I didn't feel like I'd fitted in with the kids in school really. We used to all walk to school together but I think I was too much of a tomboy for the girls, and I was too much of a girl for the boys. I was in between, trying to fit in. Even with all these people from similar areas and backgrounds to me, I just didn't fit in there either.

Once again, I felt like the outsider. I had no special friends and I used to just hang out with different people.

To this day, I cannot remember the first time that I heard about drugs. I remember hearing other children talking about them while I was still in primary school. I have memories of my friends talking about them while we played in Gals in Sheriff Street. I have a vivid memory of one of my friends talking about some of the older kids, and calling them junkies. It stands out in my mind because I didn't know what a junkie was.

We were about 11 or 12 and we'd sit down and we'd say, 'They're junkies,' as they walked down the street, but I didn't know exactly what a junkie did. I knew it was related to drugs, but I wasn't sure how.

I know now that these people were the first victims of heroin in Dublin. We weren't taught about drugs at school or anything like that. It was never ever talked about at home either.

When hard drugs hit the streets of Dublin in the mid 1980s, my family and the area I knew so well changed completely. Heroin took over.

Sheriff Street was a goldmine to sell drugs in. Everybody sold drugs there. In the past, if you saw strangers in Sheriff Street they were always watched, but now they were coming past Laurence's Mansions or from Shanahan House all the time, and it was just non-stop. The sense of community went and with it went so many lives.

I remember seeing these boys and girls all standing around doing things with their hands and going into the flats. Then they'd come back and they'd collapse. I never knew what heroin was. I didn't know what drugs were and I didn't know what they did. It was only when I left school at the age of 13 that I really found out.

Chapter 4

YOU MIGHT ASK yourself how I got into drugs given that I was so into sport. To explain how I ended up taking heroin, I need to go back to that 13-year-old kid. As we started hitting our teens, we started to go our own ways. Debbie moved out first. She had started staying in a friend's house every now and then, then she started staying away longer; she would come home after a few nights. We all had people we could stay over with, like if we were babysitting or something, but Debbie started living her own life and staying away for longer.

She had been messing around with soft drugs at this point. She met a fella and got pregnant shortly afterwards. Soon after having her son, Lee, she started taking heroin. She wasn't able to look after him as much, so Ma raised him as her own. Debbie was still involved, and she'd be with him all the time in Ma's place, but Ma thought it better if she took Lee in. Debbie wasn't much more than a child herself.

She started hanging around on Sheriff Street, where we'd always been told not to go. I followed her, cos Debbie was a very big influence on me. She was the oldest, and I looked up to her a lot. I knew she was taking drugs, but I didn't know what type or how it affected her.

Debbie used to hang around with a crowd across from the playgrounds, but when she hit this stage of her life, after having her son, she started hanging around with another gang, who were obviously into drugs. She soon turned to heroin. She was one of the first generation of heroin addicts in Dublin.

Her addiction seriously affected the family. Ma went into denial and refused to believe her daughter was a junkie, even when it became really obvious. It was only when Ma saw Debbie taking heroin, that she faced the facts. Da turned to drink.

Debbie had a lot going for her. She was very good-looking, with a great personality. Like us, she loved sport, especially tennis, and she was really good at it too. But she was wild as well. She was going to do what she wanted.

Debbie had always had her own friends, and they were all more into clothes and appearances, but I knew when she started hanging around with this new gang, that they were different to everyone else I knew. They were more mature, much older, and seemed sophisticated in ways. You could just tell they were different.

I guess they all got into drugs and that's how Debbie started using heroin. She was one of their gang. She started on heroin when she was a teenager and she was still taking heroin up to 2005 at 36 years of age. So she was on it for nearly 20 years. Thankfully she's now on a programme with Victory Outreach and is working to stay off it for good.

I eventually dropped out of school altogether. I got tired of Bosco's and I didn't want to go back to Parnell, so I started spending more time with Debbie, who had also left school by this stage. I saw that Debbie was getting in with the wrong crowd, and I got worried about her.

Debbie could be stoned but if she put on makeup and she covered up well, she could look an absolute stunner. When she was sick with gear, she looked in bits, but when she got all dolled up you'd never think she was a drug addict. Even after all the years and all the drugs that she's taken, she can still look fit and healthy.

She would take anything and everything that she could get her hands on, not just heroin. She's taken Valium and all types of drugs, both prescriptive and illegal, but still she's very outgoing and very easy to talk to.

I remember the time when things started to change. All the girls were big Madonna fans and Debbie was wearing all the Madonna-style clothes — all the raggy things in the hair, pink tops with blue ski pants, the boots and the jeans. She was really mad into all of that, and she'd go around with the big belts and the earrings. She loved clothes. Any time you seen her she was always looking at herself in the mirror, doing herself up. But then the drugs dragged her down, and she changed dramatically.

After a while, I noticed that she didn't take care of herself anymore, ever since she'd started hanging around with this other gang. Instead of hanging around with her old mates and talking about clothes or whatever, just across the way from me, she was now hanging around in Sheriff Street outside the chipper. There, and at Laurence's Mansions, was where the older crowd hung around. They were the main spots. But it was the people she was hanging around with who had changed, and that's what I noticed the most.

She stopped coming home to visit us. Although she was now living in her own flat, she spent a lot of her time at our house with the baby, but once she got involved with heroin, she'd leave the baby with Ma, but come round less and less often to see him.

All of a sudden she had a lot of fine clothes. Before she was on drugs she used to swap clothes with her other friends and she'd tell you where she got them from. Then she stopped talking to me; she wouldn't tell me where she got her clothes or anything. Everything was a secret, cos she was trying to hide it from Ma. But still I didn't know there was much of a problem cos I never actually seen her doing any drugs at that stage. I didn't understand the way she was suddenly acting.

I remember that I used to see her falling asleep and I used to say, 'Why is she falling asleep like that?' I was already an addict by the time Debbie started using in front of me.

* * * * *

There was turmoil in the family the minute drugs came along. It separated us. We weren't a family anymore. There used to be some good times when we were kids, when we'd be sitting at the table eating dinner and we'd be laughing and joking, watching Denis the Menace or the A-Team. Like any other family we'd be sitting there laughing together, but once the drugs came we'd get our dinner and couldn't wait to be gone.

We'd go into the bedroom to eat, or just scoff down the dinner and be gone out the door, cos we didn't want to be around any more. We wanted to be out with the rest of the gang, hanging around and doing whatever it was that Debbie and her mates were doing.

I thought I was old enough now to do my own thing and to hang around with whoever I wanted, wherever I wanted. Da drank more and became more and more aggressive towards us and especially towards Ma, as his frustration grew. He could see the family was falling apart and he couldn't do anything about it. We grew up and we all went our own way.

CHAPTER 5

WITH MORE TIME to myself now
that school was behind me, I was able to see
exactly what was going on in the area. With
Debbie hanging around with her new crowd
of friends, I started to hang around with more
of a gang myself. The family unit was quickly
falling apart so I realised I could get away with
a lot more. I started ignoring my parents and
turning up on Sheriff Street.

I was like any teenager, completely rebellious
and totally against all types of authority. No
one had any say in what I did any more, and
I looked instead to other people, like Debbie,
or my own friends, to show me what life was
about. And on Sheriff Street it was easy to find
ways to rebel. The most obvious way was to

start doing all the things I'd been told never to do.

I first took drugs when I was 13. I took a drag of a joint. Anyone who has ever smoked hash will probably tell you they started the same way I did, with someone passing a joint around. Not wanting to be the only one not taking a drag, I took it, and it went from there. It seemed harmless enough. Soon I was doing everything the other teenagers were doing, and I was no longer innocent to the drug culture that was taking over.

As a group, me and my mates would start smoking, and then we'd get a can of beer between loads of us and share it around. Cos we were only starting out, we'd all be drunk from drinking the one can. We knew that at night in the Alley-O, the young fellas and young ones would be there drinking two-litre flagons of cider. We'd go around to them and get a bit. So when I was 13 or 14 I knew what a joint was and I had started drinking and getting drunk.

Even though a lot of people in the area were doing drugs of some description, there was only a small group of older ones taking heroin, and for a long time you could point them out as junkies. They're nearly all dead now. We often talked about them, cos we knew what they were doing.

I'd never talk to them or anything though, cos I was afraid of them, but they made me see for myself that there were harder drugs out there and there was a dirty, sinister side to them. You couldn't really have a conversation with them anyway, because they couldn't follow what you were saying. They were spaced out and when they were drugged up, they would just sit around looking happy. When they were looking for a fix, they looked desperate and panicky. I didn't want to get into anything like that and I sure didn't want to end up like that. I don't believe that a drug addict wants to be like that. That's just the way it is for them. Surely there's no way you can be happy like that?

Even still, I kept on trying new drugs. I wasn't happy or fulfilled in my life and I realised that smoking dope and hanging around in the crowd gave me something to do. Then dance music came along and changed my world.

All my friends started going to the nightclubs that were playing dance music and it was amazing. The dance beat is about the same pace as your heart beat and it was so easy to get caught up in the music. Hash was no good for this though, because it made me mellow, so when I discovered ecstasy, I thought I was in heaven.

I was around 16 when I first took an ecstasy tablet. No one has ever named a drug so appropriately. The first time I took it I danced for around seven hours. I was always energetic because of the football, but this gave me a new sense of invincibility.

I got addicted to the highs of ecstasy, and every weekend, my mates and I would go to different clubs around Dublin. The party scene got me deep into the drug culture. We went all over the country looking for a good time. We used to go down to Cork on a Friday night and I wouldn't come back until Sunday. I'd be wired to the moon. This is where my life started going downhill. I went on to use LSD, Valium and anything else I could lay my hands on. These were the first 'hard' drugs I took.

The girls I hung around with were a bit more advanced in their drug taking than I was, though I caught up fast. They introduced me to all these types of drugs.

It might sound strange but I was still doing sport at this stage. Sport was actually associated with drugs for me. We'd sit on the roof and smoke a joint while watching a match. Some of the fellas playing the match would be smoking a joint and then walking onto the pitch.

* * * * *

When I was going partying I knew heroin was going around, and cos I could see what was happening to Debbie, turning from a popular, good looking girl into a heroin addict, I said I wasn't going to go near that stuff.

I could hear people calling her a junkie, and I hated it, but it wasn't long before I called her a junkie myself. There'd be big fights about it between us. Up until this point, I could only see the negative side to heroin. No one told me the good things. No one told me heroin's little secret.

Heroin is a unique drug. You could say it's the most beautiful drug in the world. You could also say it's the most disgusting drug in the world. It depends on your point of view. But there really is nothing like it.

Initially when you take heroin, it takes you away from reality. I don't know how to explain just how good it feels. It's hard to describe it. Can you imagine feeling every good sensation known to man at the same time? Can you imagine feeling happy, fulfilled, self-confident and loved all at once? Heroin gives you a false sense of reality and confidence. You could be looking like a dog, and yet, heroin will tell you that you look good.

I would learn that heroin makes you feel this way; it is the ultimate drug. It's the ultimate form of escape. It gives you a reason to live. It can also give you a reason to die. It can be your best friend or your worst enemy, or sometimes, it can be both at once. Above all, it gives you a lot of false confidence.

Heroin befriended me when no one else did and it gave me much happiness before taking my life away. I was one of the lucky ones. I took my life back.

People like you often ask why people like me started taking heroin. The answer is simple; it was a moment of weakness. It could happen to you. Don't be fooled into thinking that heroin is contained within the working-classes.

I know people from all walks of life who have ended up taking heroin. Someone like you could end up on heroin if you happened to be caught off guard.

After all the terrible things I had seen heroin do; after all the promises I made myself to stay away from the 'dirty drug', I had no idea that one night at a party I would be offered some heroin, and under the influence of ecstasy, I'd take it.

CHAPTER 6

I FOUND OUT what the phrase 'Chasing the Dragon' meant that first night. This means that I smoked heroin, using tin foil and a tooter. Forgive the use of terminology, but you'll get used to it.

I was high on ecstasy that night. I'd been at a nightclub in town and taken about three strong ecstasy pills, and then went back to a party in Laurence's Mansions. I was so wired I thought I'd never be able to relax and come down, and I'd never be able to sleep. When I got there I knew some heroin was going around. I was watching it being passed around and I knew it was eventually going to come to me.

I was sitting there for what felt like a million years watching this, and all the time I was debating what I was going to do. I was telling myself to look at Debbie and see what it had done to her.

I was fighting with my conscience, saying 'don't take it, don't take it', but it was like there was an angel sitting on one shoulder and the devil sitting on the other, arguing over what to do. In the end, the devil won.

The fella I was with at the time took it, and I was next in line. He set it all up for me. He took the tin foil and burned it underneath with the dull part up. Everyone's hands get filthy when they do this, so he had to wipe his hands with toilet paper afterwards. He then rolled a bit of the foil up around a cigarette or a pen — that was the tooter — and then he burned underneath the heroin for a minute to melt it into liquid, before he handed it to me to inhale the smoke through the tooter. I didn't think about it at this point; I just took it. I inhaled the heroin through the tooter. I then took a drag off a joint and held it in for as long as I could. It was horrible.

The heroin was sickening, and I soon discovered that it leaves these horrible marks on your teeth like little black spots of resin. It tasted foul to me that first time, and I got sick everywhere. The thing was, unfortunately for me, it worked. I'm sorry to say that.

I would hate to say I liked it cos that would sound like I'm saying drugs are good for you, but it did the trick for me that night cos I was so high, needing to come down off the ecstasy trip. That's what the heroin did. It made me sleepy. You can't sleep after ecstasy. You have to take Valium or heroin to come down off it.

Smoking hash or drinking doesn't work. As soon as I took the heroin, I was drowsy and wanted to go to sleep, and after I got sick, I felt a lot better.

* * * * *

I ended up getting a little bag of heroin every time I got ecstasy, to bring me down after a night out. It was a weekend thing for me. I'd go out clubbing, take Es, smoke some heroin at four or five in the morning and go to sleep. The problem was that it became a Monday and a Tuesday thing very soon, then a Wednesday, Thursday and Friday thing. Eventually, I stopped taking Es and just took heroin. I liked the feeling cos it blocked out everything and made me forget my worries and the problems I was having at home.

The girls I was taking ecstasy with started to blank me after a few weeks. They were looking down on me cos, as they said, they were on the white powder, but I was on the brown powder. To them, it was okay to take ecstasy and cocaine but I was a dirty junkie. Cocaine was the rich person's drug. Taking it meant you were a different class of person.

I'd started taking more drugs, trying to fit in, to feel like I belonged somewhere, and now that I was taking them every day, I felt I was being pushed out again. So I stopped hanging around with them after a while. I was sick of being looked down at by people taking as much drugs as I was.

I started going to a place in town, a day-care clinic where all the junkies hung out. It's closed now, but at the time you'd be able to just go in there and goof off all day. That became my day. I'd get some heroin, go to the centre, drink tea and smoke and sit there all day talking about all the things I didn't have. All I remember saying is, 'I wish this' and, 'I wish that' and I'd end up just sitting there stoned.

Yet heroin still wasn't that commonplace. Yes, a lot of the people I hung around with would smoke it, but few were shooting up. The ones who were using it all the time were well-known. Debbie was hanging around with the dealers, so I knew she was still taking it. Everyone knew the dealers. People would come from the north side and the south side to Sheriff Street to buy heroin off them. They're all dead now too, the ones who brought it into the area in the first place. They either overdosed or died of AIDS, or killed themselves.

I was getting pretty street smart so my family didn't realise for ages that I was taking serious drugs. I used to always say I was staying in someone else's house for the night, like Debbie used to do, and I'd send someone around to tell Ma. She started getting suspicious, and kept asking to see my arms, to see if she could find needle marks. She never found any, but she saw enough in my behaviour to know that I was up to something. She had no doubt I was taking drugs.

In the end, she took a very brave step and decided to go and ask for help for me. She put my name down for the drug clinic on Amiens Street. I was annoyed when she did this, but

I went anyway just because I promised her. When I went in, it was pretty obvious to them that I was an addict. I got assessed and was put on a dosage of physeptone, or phy as we called it, which was an early version of methadone. We called this Brown, and it was strong.

There was a lot of sugar in it, so it made you lose your teeth. There are loads of ex-junkies out there with false teeth because of it. Phy is much harder to come off than heroin. Now, you can get what they call Green, which is methadone, and it's like diet phy because it's sugar free.

* * * * *

You may be wondering how I financed my drug habit, since I obviously wasn't working. I'm ashamed to say that I ended up becoming a thief to support my habit, and then later, a drugs courier.

I started shoplifting but I was never into violent crime. I was probably worse than some of the fellas, but I never robbed a handbag. I never did anything like that. My conscience stopped me, cos I used to think I wouldn't like anybody to do that to Ma, to rob her handbag. I'd often see fellas at Joseph's Mansions, at the traffic lights, or on Amiens or Sheriff Street, and they'd just smash a car window and rob some poor woman's handbag off the seat beside her. The woman would be sitting there screaming and I'd have that picture in my head all day.

I was a disaster at shoplifting though. If I took something it would be written all over my face, 'I just robbed something from your shop!' One girl I was with, oh my God, she was a good shoplifter. But I was bad. She used to just kick me out of the shop out of frustration. I knew I was doing it wrong.

When I was robbing something on somebody, somewhere in the back of my head I was thinking, 'This is not right. I shouldn't be doing this.' And because I was feeling like that, even though I'd be out of my head, the guilt would be all over my face. I'm really shy and I wouldn't do anything intentionally to hurt anybody. That's not my character. My character is real soft and I'm easy to get on with. Robbing just doesn't suit me at all. I'd be red with embarrassment going out of the shop, and the security would know straight away what I was up to. They'd never even have to say anything to me other than, 'C'mon, you're going.' It was so obvious.

The first time I robbed something I was caught. I was only a kid and it was long before I got into drugs. I think I only did it cos all my mates were doing it. I was after robbing a copybook or something out of Eason's. We were all doing it that day cos we were on the mitch from school.

I was brought home by the police, and as soon as they left I got battered, absolutely kicked around, by Ma and Da. Shoplifting definitely wasn't my forte. It involved too many people. It took me an hour to rob a jacket, and the big shops like Arnott's used to frighten the life out of me. Running out the back door in Arnott's was the best way to do it. Even though we got away most of the time, afterwards I'd be like, 'Oh, that was hard,' while my mates thought it was easy. But it was hard for me.

We'd go in and just take loads of things. Levi jeans were the best, cos they were so dear, and everybody wanted them. You'd get about four or five pairs, stick them in a bag, and run out the door. We might take a pair each, or sell them together, split the money, and go our separate ways. Then it was like, 'See you later' and that was that. You would never hang around with a particular person for too long. You always moved around and worked with somebody different.

I shoplifted with that girl and her sister on and off for years. They're related to some big name criminals.

Back then, shoplifting wasn't difficult. Now, they have an anti-theft device where the paint comes out and the clothes are no good. Back then they didn't have any alarms on the doors. They had security guards but they used to be at the front door only. Sometimes I'd go in the shop and I'd start messing around and touching everything just to sidetrack the security guard, while my friends went in and robbed loads of clothes. I'd just walk around the shop and the security guard would follow me everywhere, while they'd be fleecing the place.

Christmas was the best time for me. It was a relief. I didn't have a problem cos there was no way you could rob. They would watch everybody going in and out of the shops, so it meant we had no chance to take anything. But that was an exception. Most of the time, I was off my face and robbing.

Even after a few years, I still wasn't up for the robbing life though. I remember some really embarrassing incidents. I robbed Spice Girls dolls, and I nearly got caught. I was even embarrassed at the time, thinking to myself, 'What am I doing robbing Spice Girls dolls?' But they were popular and I was getting £20 for them. They were expensive enough. And so I said I'd rob them.

I took the black one — Scary Spice. I just grabbed them and was just gone out the door of the shop. It was horrible though, cos I nearly got caught. Imagine that — getting charged and all that; being put in prison for robbing Spice Girls dolls.

Chapter 7

I WAS BOUND to end up in jail. It didn't take long, the way I was going. In fact, I went to jail twice. The first time I was on remand for two weeks and the second time it was for six months. I was put away for shoplifting, as you might have guessed. You don't get locked up for what you actually took on the day, you get locked up for your previous convictions, and they were weeding them out the day I went in.

The first time I was sent away, I wasn't actually on heroin; I was on phy and I was supposed to be trying to get off heroin. I continued to shoplift though and I got lifted for it, charged and brought to court.

I knew it was going to happen to me. I had several convictions from when I was a teenager, but I had never spent any time behind bars. When I was finally sent down, it all seemed a little unreal. The judge said, 'Miss O'Toole, you've a lot of previous convictions.' He asked me if there was anybody in court with me. I said there wasn't.

My solicitor kept saying, 'Well Miss O'Toole has a drug problem and she's hoping to go into this and that.' He was trying to keep me out of jail, because I was in a heap.

At the time I couldn't even think about going to jail. I think he knew if I'd have gone to Mountjoy for a long stretch that I'd have been dead. I wouldn't have survived it, because it's such a horrible place.

The judge said, 'Well, I don't care if she's trying to get herself off drugs. It's not my problem that she's doing *this*. She can't be doing that. I'm going to remand this case for two weeks and that's it.'

I just stood there in shock. Although I had been breaking the law, for some reason it didn't occur to me that I might go to jail for it.

It was really horrible, knowing I was going to prison. They put me in handcuffs and I stayed in the Bridewell all day, till the rest of the prisoners were processed and finished with their hearings. When everybody was ready to go they put me and the others in what they call the meat wagon. It's like the Brinks vans, only it is full of people going to jail. You just stand there. There is a little seat but it's so small there's no way you could sit on it. It's a horrible atmosphere. There's loads of young kids going to Saint Patrick's and loads of young women and girls going to Mountjoy. I think those vans hold about eight or 12 people, and none of them are going anywhere nice.

Back then, the women's prison in Mountjoy wasn't anything like it is now. It was scary, especially to the likes of me. I was still a teenager. I was only 19. I felt like a little girl caught up in all this madness. I didn't know what I was doing. Heroin controlled me. It dictated what I did, who I was with and who I did it with. I didn't know what I was doing with my life, and now, suddenly, I found myself in Mountjoy Prison.

When we went in, it was really rough. The screws all looked very tough. Some of them looked evil. I thought they were going to kill me every time they looked at me. We had to take off all our clothes together. The guards were all just standing there. They put a kind of a cloak, like a nightdress or something, over us and you had to stand there being stared at, and then they strip searched you. There were four women there. One of them would be getting your clothes ready, the others just stood there looking us up and down.

They strip-searched me with gloves. I wasn't sure if they were going to search me internally, but I was relieved when they didn't. They just searched my mouth, ears, and my hair.

At least they didn't do the whole search in front of the other prisoners. We were brought in one by one, but the other screws all had a good look. They'd take the cloak off you and make you stand there while they'd do the strip search. When that was finished they'd put you in the shower. Then they'd give you some clothes. Because you'd be on remand you didn't know if you were going to get locked up or not, so you had to wear what they gave you.

It's not like that now. I remember the little cabin we were in. I'll never forget it. Now, any time I see a train or anything like that it reminds me of the cabins. My friend has a caravan down in Donabate, and when I walk into it, it reminds me so much of that cabin. I just remember being there and getting in the shower, terrified. I don't even think I washed myself right. I was shaking with fear and embarrassment. Having them look at me with no clothes on was mortifying. They were just looking at me, not even saying anything, just staring.

I remember feeling desperate when I was having that first shower. They pulled the curtains back and there I was, just crying and crying. When I was finished, another prisoner came in and took her turn in the shower. I found it degrading.

I just didn't understand why the screws were standing there looking at me like they were, and some of them were laughing. It felt like they were mocking me. 'She thinks she's it now, she's in our hands now, we'll see what she's made of.'

They knew what I was like, cos they thought, 'You're not in prison because you're a good girl.' They were ready to teach us a lesson.

As I got out of the shower they gave me some underwear, toothpaste and all the essential stuff, and then sent me into the prison.

I recognised people I knew from Sheriff Street, some of my shoplifting friends. One of them gave me clothes. When you're on remand you're allowed visits but you're not allowed to get any clothes from home. You have to wear the prison clothing, which was terrible. All of the remand prisoners were put in a wing together on the first landing. It was horrible.

Remands stay on their own, so I was brought to my own cell. The door was shut and I was left there. You are not allowed to mix with the prisoners until that evening or the next day — it depends on what time you come in at. I didn't see anybody until the next morning.

I sat there all night scared. You hear all these stories about prison and what happens to you when you first go in, like they're going to gang rape you, or they're going to kill you, and cut your hair and do all sorts of things to you. I didn't know what to believe, but having to shower together and not knowing what would happen next was one of my worst fears. I decided to keep my head down and wait for my release.

You had to see the doctor the morning after you went in. I told her my story, what I was taking and how I visited the clinic every day. She gave me methadone and sleeping tablets and that was it. I was an inmate then. I figured I had my maintenance and my own cell and that that's where I'd stay. I didn't actually mix at all in Mountjoy at that time.

I convinced myself it would get easier so I kept quiet, stayed in my cell, and did the two weeks quietly but it didn't get any easier.

At the time I was upset and was praying to God for help. I wasn't really religious but when you're in trouble you turn to God, don't you?

'Get me out of this and I won't do it again, I swear. I promise you! I'll go to church on Christmas and all, I will! You'll see me there, I'll go!'

I was making all sorts of promises, crying my eyes out. And the thing is; I think everybody behind the doors of Mountjoy cries. When they turn the lock, I think that people find it very hard to cope. I know I did.

Even though I was an energetic and happy kind of person, deep down I was hurting. I was sad and depressed and I just felt like there was no hope for me. When the doors closed, that's when I really had a look at myself and thought, 'What am I doing here?'

Apart from the gym, there were no activities in prison at that time but I never went in to it during the entire two weeks that I was there. I was too scared. Today they have school classes and art and drama projects. You can go out and do things, but it wasn't like that when I was there. Everybody was just hanging around the landings, going into each other's cells and just doing nothing really. Even though I knew people, I didn't mix with them. I was too into myself. The drugs did this to me.

After the two weeks on remand I returned to court. The judge said I had to prove I was trying to do something with my life. The solicitor told the judge that I was a drug addict and that I came from a family of eight kids, and there were problems at home. She said Ma and Da didn't work and Da was a drinker. Ma this and Da that . . .

He was trying to prevent a custodial sentence. So the judge remanded me on bail and said to me that I was to improve and try to get better. So I had to go to a course on the Anna Livia Project, where I was to get help to come off the drugs. I would have agreed to anything to get out of Mountjoy, but I don't think I ever really believed I was going to recover and give up drugs for good.

The Anna Livia Project was a programme for recovering addicts that tried to show the damage heroin was doing, not only to them but to the community. They also tried to get you off heroin or any other drug you were on, but that was done gradually. I wouldn't have gone at all myself, but I had to go to prove to the court that I was trying to change. I was just trying to do something, anything to avoid going back to jail.

I went to France with them for what they called the Irish French Drug Programme. It took place in the north of France in a place called Lille. We were to do a course on how drug addicts get over their habit.

Occasionally I got by without heroin, but only for a while. Whenever I was off heroin, I needed my maintenance. I couldn't get by without phy. I didn't do heroin during those two weeks in France because I couldn't.

The strange thing was that it was easy enough to stay off it. I wasn't in pain because I had plenty of phy with me. The Anna Livia Project wrote letters for us, saying that we were going away for a certain amount of time and we needed to take our 'takeaways' with us. So that's what we did. You'd never drink all your phy yourself when you know you're going away for two weeks, so I had more than enough, and Lille was a lovely place. I didn't know how it was supposed to help me though. I brought loads of hash with me. The people on the programme didn't know. I couldn't get heroin there because I was afraid of getting caught.

When I came back I went up to the Anna Livia every afternoon. I had to have a report saying that I was going to it, and I had to show this to the solicitor when I was back in court. The solicitor then told the court that I was working on my addiction and that I had clean urine etc.

On paper it looked good, and I went along with it for a while, but then I just went back to being a druggy. I got bored with it because it wasn't enough.

Being in prison on remand should have terrified me into changing my life, but it didn't. I just went straight back to doing what I always did. I had to do the Anna Livia course and all that but I was just treading water. I did think about things for a while, but it didn't frighten me. In a way it was kind of like, 'Yeah, I was in prison . . . deadly!'

And then when I got out everybody was asking me for stories, saying, 'Oh, what's it like in there, what's it like?' I was living up to it, playing hard and telling lies. To this day I wonder what was going through my head. I had some stupid conversations with other users.

'Oh, it's deadly. Easy, you know what I mean? Easy! Do time any day'

I used to lie, saying I could have done it on my back. I did do it on my back — on my back crying.

And I did it rough. I never came out of my cell that first time cos I was so afraid. In prison it's like there's this thing going on, they call it the prison buzz. Some people are into it, and they know the ropes. They know everything. Others don't, and never get into it.

It's like the drugs buzz. It's like a little world on its own. Some people know how the system works and they know when somebody smuggles drugs into the jail; they are after them like a shot. It's like they own the prison and they're standing on the corner of the C wing waiting for you, saying, 'All right?'

You'd think they were standing in the street. It's just a prison buzz, being wide to everything, running the place, and a lot of the women are into it.

And then you have some women who do their time in the gym. They go to the gym and sit there all day. These women don't mix with anybody and they just do their time. They put their head down and they get stuck into the gym or a project or something like that.

Some of the new inmates think they're on Sheriff Street or Sean MacDermott Street. No one really understands this attitude unless they've been inside.

* * * * *

By the time I got back from France, I had gotten used to the phy that the Amiens Street clinic was supplying, and I started looking for another buzz. I quickly went back to heroin. This meant I was now doing two hard drugs at once, keeping up two habits. They used to do urine tests on me at the clinic, to make sure I was staying off heroin. But there were ways around that. All you had to do was get someone else's clean urine. You'd go into the cubicle and wait a minute, then flush the toilet and come out, handing them someone else's sample. I used to give them a clean sample every time.

Looking back on it now, one of the biggest mistakes of my life was going to that clinic. It just wasn't for me. Before it, I'd only smoked heroin, and was surrounded by people my own age doing the same thing. Now, I found myself hanging around with older, more experienced people who'd been doing drugs and going to the clinics for years. They had been transferred from Baggot Street or Pearse Street. They got thrown off their course of rehab or they were transferred, as punishment, to somewhere far from their normal haunts. That's what they did at the clinics. They'd send you to a different clinic if they got a dirty urine sample from you.

I know they were trying to help us, but all I got from the clinic was the chance to meet a lot of older addicts. I know it works for others, but it didn't for me. In no time, I started taking tablets, and then a lot more than that.

All of these addicts knew the ropes, and they were asking me why I didn't mainline. After smoking heroin for a while, you start to look at everyone else injecting it and it starts to make sense. I was a chronic addict at this stage but I found it almost impossible to get a rush. It took ages to get a buzz when I just smoked heroin, but using a needle was supposed to give you a better, longer high.

As I was hanging around with these people, while I was trying to get high, I'd see them lying around wasted. I wanted to be one of them I suppose, to be part of their group. I decided I wasn't going to waste a whole bag of heroin smoking it anymore. So it wasn't long before I was injecting it. My new friends showed me how.

I remember the first time I used a needle. You start off by 'skin-popping'. This is where you pinch a bit of skin to raise it, and just stick the needle in. We used very thin needles for this, similar to the ones used by diabetics. It takes about twenty minutes to take effect, but you know all about it when it does. After that, it's only a matter of time before you move onto mainlining into your veins.

I nearly killed myself the first time I skin-popped. I was out cold. But the feeling of the heroin going into my veins was much better than smoking it but it just knocked me out. I had some fella inject me in a toilet, and I remember I just had to sit down straight away.

It was a big rush to my head and it was like my whole body shut down. I was in another world, so high. I was completely out of it.

This actually happened in Debbie's flat, and she didn't like it. She was saying, 'No, don't show her how to do it that way,' but I insisted. She would do the same on the street. She'd tell people not to sell heroin to me if she saw me trying to score. After a while though, when she saw it was going to happen anyway, she gave up. I moved in with her for a few months then, and we ended up shooting up together.

At this stage I was becoming more and more involved in the drug culture and in crime. I needed money to pay for my habit, so I ended up dealing and shoplifting. The whole area was going downhill at the same rate I was, and the dealers were making a killing, taking advantage of a huge market.

I knew the people involved — the dealers and the addicts — so I got into it, running drugs. I wasn't involved in everything at first — just heroin and hash. I'd started off with hash, but you progress.

All along Sheriff Street there was dealing going on, but it was mainly in Joseph's Mansions that I did my business. I was up and down the stairs so much it was unbelievable. People would come along and give me money, and I'd take it up to the fella that I was doing it for, and then bring the drugs back down.

There were times when people wouldn't believe that I was going to bring it back down, but never once when I was doing that for him did I rip anybody off. I never took their money and didn't come back, cos dealing for this fella was my way of getting a bag of gear. I got paid in bags of gear for doing what I did.

I depended on drug dealing for myself. I didn't want to jeopardise that in a way, that I couldn't get my gear off him. That's what the whole thing was. It was like an agreement. I was running up and down to this guy with money and bringing the heroin down in tiny bags to the customers.

At the end of the day, I got my gear and he had his money. There was never much of a risk. The heroin was so tightly wrapped, you'd think it was just a big ball of chewing gum, but it was about six or seven bags of gear.

When you have the drugs and people know you are involved, you suddenly know a lot of people. I'd know people from the Southside and the Northside. I'd know people from one end of the city to the other. Even to this day, I couldn't walk through town without bumping into somebody that I sold drugs to, or somebody that I had a 'turn-on' with. That was the thing — it wasn't only people from Sheriff Street that came to Joseph's Mansions. People came from all over the city.

As I went on I met fellas and girls that were taking drugs for years, and they knew what they were doing. I began to learn from these people. They were keen to get me in on it. So I just learnt as I went along and every day was different; two days were never the same. There was always somebody different to meet. Different faces, different situations. The only thing that stayed the same was the drugs, and the line of people waiting to get them. Drugs was what we had in common. You could talk to somebody and say, 'All right? What's the story?' and all that. But really you had nothing in common. It was just drugs. They just took heroin, same as you, or they bought hash, and so in the end, that's what you'd talk about.

My average day back then was fairly ordinary and it was easy to get into a routine. I'd try to get up in time to go to the clinic on Amiens Street. I knew it shut at around noon at the latest, so I had to be up before then. If you missed the clinic you'd have to wait for the next day. There were a lot of different people going in to the clinic, all in different stages of dependency and sickness. There were people that just went in and got by for the day, but then sometimes there were people that were getting a three-day fix. They'd go there twice a week or on weekends. They'd get their dosage to last them all week and they'd just have to go at weekends to collect their physeptone.

But when I started going to the clinic I was going every day. I'd go to the clinic, and hang around outside for a couple of hours afterwards. I was with this fella at the time and he wasn't due in until a quarter to one, so I'd wait on him. When he finished, we'd probably go to the day care centre, just hanging out there, and then I'd go to Joseph's Mansions. I wouldn't even try to sell drugs till late afternoon. There would be no point until then, cos you'd have no customers yet.

They'd all be out trying to get their money, doing whatever they did to get it. Mostly it meant they were up the town shoplifting, out robbing handbags or whatever.

Joseph's Mansions, up off Buckingham Street, became the centre for all of the dealers. Mary's Mansions was busy as well. After one or two in the afternoon the place would be buzzing. There'd be people all over the place, all of them either buying or selling drugs. After a while though, the residents managed to get rid of all of the dealers and addicts out of Mary's Mansions, and then they shifted onto Sheriff Street, but Sheriff Street itself wasn't the best place for junkies either. This was because there were people living there who were prepared to fight the wave of pushers and dealers — vigilantes and anti-drugs campaigners — so a lot of it stopped.

Joseph's Mansions was a different story altogether though. The place was a magnet for junkies. If you were looking for somebody, you'd find him at Joseph's Mansions. If you weren't a junkie, you tended to stay away. If you were looking to buy some gear, you knew you could go in and there'd be no vigilantes stopping you. There was always a bottom flat in there where you could go and get stoned and smoke gear. You'd sit there all day, just nodding off. There were times when I didn't know what happened to my bike or where it was, and I needed it to get up and down the streets all day. I'd end up in one of those rooms and I wouldn't remember what I done with it that evening. I always got it back in the end though. Everybody knew it belonged to me.

I suppose sometimes it could be a bit dangerous hanging around these places, especially if you didn't know many of the people who came in from outside Sheriff Street. Sometimes I'd meet people and they'd say, 'What are you doing, do you want to come for a smoke?' I'd go with them sometimes, thinking they just wanted company, or maybe just wanting some company myself, but I didn't get into the habit of it with strangers. The way I saw it, once I was inside one of them flats and there were drugs around to take, I didn't care who I was with.

We used to call the flats behind Sean MacDermott Street's church the Dead Flats. So many people had died in there from drugs. On the bottom of the block there was a flat that was always just full of junkies. I don't even know who owned it. It was all bricked up on the outside but at the back you could get in. It wasn't long before there were places like that in most flat complexes. The complexes were all getting knocked down at this point and people were moving into small council estates nearby. They were a no-go area for everybody but us.

There was never any electricity in these places. Just candles. We'd just sit in there and get stoned. There'd be young fellas lying on the ground inside these flats, completely out of their heads. That's where you went if you wanted to have a turn-on, to shoot up. You could have a smoke on the stairs in Joseph's Mansions, but if you wanted to have a turn-on, even though some people did on the stairs, the Dead Flats was where you went. That's where I used to go.

I'd got into a sort of lifestyle that was easy. I'd just go to the clinic, buzz around town for a while, see what the story was with getting drugs, and then I'd go down and sell heroin for your man. It was worry free. No hassle.

People would come in, get what they wanted, and get out again. It was real quick. A fella off the telly came down one day. He was an actor. He came down on a motorbike looking for hash. That was how we knew that everybody knew what was going on.

I'd ask myself, 'How could he know about it, he's not from around here?' He'd be from over the Southside somewhere, this fella. I don't want to say who he is. But there he was. Pulled up on a bike!

It was obvious that it wasn't just the people from Sheriff Street who were buying and selling now. There were all different types of people coming to score the same things we were using. There was a lot of heroin sold, and a lot of hash, but there was also coke. And then you had all the E-heads. It was a constant flow of customers — all different types of people wanting different types of drugs. And you could get them all in the one place.

Everywhere you looked someone was using, buying or selling drugs. The situation was getting out of control. And so was I. As well as Valium, I started taking whatever else I could get my hands on, including drugs that were used for cancer patients. These were serious drugs. They made me hallucinate and nervous. I'd get stoned from them but I'd just wake up in the morning and I wouldn't know what I was after doing. I was just like my Da. I'd no idea what I was doing sometimes.

One night I took about 20 of these tablets and I was sitting with Ma and her friend in the kitchen. I was after taking these tablets when I was out somewhere, but I'd gone home afterwards because they always made me want to talk — to anyone. I kept saying to Ma's friend, 'Here, come on. We'll have a turn-on, me Ma's not watching,' and I started taking out the needles and the spoons and started getting water, preparing everything so we could shoot up.

Ma just beat the head off me and started screaming all over the place. I was that bad I didn't know she was standing there!

CHAPTER 8

BY THIS TIME, I fell further and further into my drug addiction. I did a lot of things I wouldn't normally do in order to pay for it. Some people did try to help me. There was one garda, who I think is in the drugs squad now. She was only a rookie then, and she really tried to make me see sense. I knew her through my sister, Olivia, so she knew who I was and would always say to my sister, 'What's Julie doing; can you not help her?'

When I'd meet Olivia, she used to say to me, 'She's asking about you. What are you doing? She said you should get away from them friends of yours. You're ruining your life.'

I think this garda understood the problems I was facing. She knew the dealers I was working for. She also knew they were scumbags. I think she felt sorry for people like me who got caught up in it. Because I was on the other side of the fence, I thought she was just like every other garda, even though she was just doing her job, and looking out for me. Heroin makes you think that way. I now know that she was actually trying to help me, but I couldn't see it at the time, and I wanted nothing to do with her.

The funny thing is that she never actually said it to my face, but a couple of times she came up to Ma's house and she'd just look at me, nodding her head in my direction. She knew that I was an addict by just looking at me. But I think that she thought I was better than that. She knew I was good at football and that I gave it up after I started taking drugs. I'm sure when she looked at me she thought, 'What is she doing with her life?'

I think she saw that I had the potential to do anything, but that I was destroying my life.

The garda would have been around the same age as Olivia, but our lives couldn't have been more different. She was a good garda — the sort of woman that takes her job seriously.

At the time, she was a community officer, and she saw how heroin had destroyed the inner city. She saw what we couldn't — the devastation and the despair. Her job was to get rid of us, to stop what we were doing. Of course, I never saw it that way at the time.

I still see her now and she continues to be involved in community issues. I stop and talk to her now and she still asks when I am going to start playing football again.

* * * * *

Running drugs was never about making money. It was all about just getting enough so I could buy more drugs. I'd no interest in anything else anymore. Sport went out the window. I looked awful and smelt rotten.

Dealing and running the drugs came naturally after a while. I'd watched enough people do it. As I told you, I didn't decide one day, 'Okay, I'm going to be a drug addict,' and in the same way, I never started out thinking I was going to make a career out of running or selling drugs.

I often laugh at this picture of my First Holy Communion. I was so innocent then.

Left: When I went to France on a drug treatment programme, I made sure I took plenty of hash with me.

The organizers knew nothing about it, but I was too afraid to take heroin through customs.

Above: We had to share the one bedroom between us when we lived in Laurence's Flats.

Left: My parents didn't want me hanging around Sheriff Street when I was a teenager, but I did anyway, even though the place had become a slum.

We're still close as a family, and we can have a laugh when we all get together. We've had some good memories, like seeing Olivia playing for Ireland. We're her biggest fans (below).

When I was on heroin I could never have imagined that today I'd be clean, healthy, and helping others get through their addiction. I have a new life and I'm looking forward to spending the rest of it with my loving family, and my husband, Gerard. Eighteen months ago my dream of having my own family came true with the birth of my son.

I actually knew nothing about it when I started. I just learnt the trade as I went along. Like an apprentice, I learnt it from the people around me. I continued to distribute drugs for the dealers in my area. Ferrying heroin around the streets kept me going. I had no other way of making money. I would cycle around with wraps of smack hidden in my mouth. The gardaí had come to know me and I was often stopped and searched.

But they never caught me with anything. At the time, they didn't know that we carried heroin in our mouths. I always hid it in the roof of my mouth, or right behind my back teeth. No one ever knew that's where I kept it. I could still talk when I was stopped and searched, so I could give them all the talk they wanted and I'd never give myself away. If there was a female garda with them she was allowed to search in your mouth and she'd put her hand in and feel around. If you didn't have the nerve, or you couldn't hide it in your mouth well, you would either have to spit it out or you'd swallow it, depending on how much you had.

I never carried anything so big that I had to swallow it or spit it out; it always fitted neatly on the back of my gums. I think this infuriated the gardaí. They would see me cycling around and they knew what I was doing but they could never find the evidence.

The truth was that we were our own little community of druggies. No one knew how we did our business. We never did anything with anyone outside our own circle. Even though I was an addict, I managed to run drugs like a proper little business. I worked the streets. All of us worked the streets. We'd hear about things from other junkies. If someone was caught robbing or dealing, we'd hear about it fast.

I never read about anything in the newspapers, but I'd hear about it from someone. These things were treated as a joke.

'Did you hear what happened to yer man?' and all that. If it was a big thing, it would be big news for the day. If somebody was caught joyriding a car, out of their head, and ploughed into the wall — that would be something to talk about. If they died it would be a different story, of course. But I was never aware of how serious these things were. To be honest, I just never thought about it. And we never thought about anything that didn't affect us.

We had our community and nothing outside really influenced it. That's really sad, isn't it? But that's how it was. I can honestly say the only thing that I ever thought about was heroin. It was all that mattered to me.

It's like you're living on a little island and it's just you and your mates. I never thought about it that way. It's funny. I never even knew that parts of Dublin existed until I got off drugs.

* * * * *

I soon found myself locked up for six months again. I was only out of jail for three months when I was caught shoplifting again. I was a repeat offender, so as soon as I got in trouble, it was straight back into the 'Joy.

The judge said that I had my chance and that there were consequences for what I had done. He said I didn't take the opportunity he gave me. I knew he was right, but what could I say? I just put my head down. I knew in my heart; I knew that I'd made a huge mistake.

I was going to prison now and not getting out for a long time. I started to cry as soon as the judge sentenced me.

I went through the same process as before. When I was taken into the jail, I got strip searched, showered, and all that. The first time was kind of unreal, like it was not really happening. The first time I was only on remand. But the second time I was really a prisoner, and I was put into a cell with other girls. I started screaming, 'Get me out of this cell, get me out of this cell!'

There were three of us in the cell. Sometimes these girls could be a great laugh, but if you got on the wrong side of them, they'd eat you.

I remember lying there one night and thinking to myself. I knew my life was going really bad, but I didn't know how to get out of it.

Ma came to see me the next morning. I broke down when I saw her. I remember screaming across the dividing bar. 'Ma, get me out of here!'

Every day on the phone I was the same, 'Ma, please get me out of here.'

'I can't get you out.'

It was as simple as that. I had to serve my time.

Ma brought me some clothes — I was allowed to have my own clothes cos I was a real inmate this time.

* * * * *

I remember the prison regime well. You got up at a quarter past eight, went down, got your breakfast and brought it back to your cell. You ate it in your cell back then. They don't anymore. Now they have this big canteen where they all sit together. A lot of the drug users would just go down for tea because nobody ate early in the morning. We were all drug addicts, and drug addicts don't eat until late at night. The cell door would be opened at a quarter past nine and you'd be out, standing in the yard smoking, messing with a ball or something, or sitting in the gym; just talking about nothing. It was usually all big talk. People saying, 'We used to do this, and we used to do that and I used to do this and I used to do that.' You know all that rubbish.

I hated that. Some of the inmates would be telling stories all the time, saying, 'Ah yeah, we robbed this and we got this.'

Then they used to say to me, 'Have you any toothpaste on you?

'Oh, you'll give us a cigarette, will ya?'

The girls would talk about how much money they had made robbing, and how many thousands of pounds they had waiting on them outside, but they wouldn't even have the basics in jail. Some of them felt the need to keep the hard image up, even though it was obvious they were prisoners just like me.

At a quarter past one you'd be locked up for your lunch and at two o'clock you were let back out. Then you're out all day, and you'd be just doing nothing. Absolutely nothing. If you were in the laundry; if you were doing your clothes, you'd sit there and wait.

If you're in the gym you just do whatever you want. Some people use the gym and some young ones just stand there laughing and messing around. You were out of your cell all day till a quarter past five.

I didn't mix with all the prisoners — just the townies. As far as I was concerned, there was travellers, country people, townies, and then there was the Southsiders. You also had all these muppets running around, from all over the shop. They didn't really fit in with anyone.

We were locked up at seven until the next morning. And everybody was all right until seven o'clock hit. It was all, 'Give us a smoke!' and, 'See you tomorrow morning!' on the landing, as if they didn't have a care in the world. The thing is, while it was all smiles on the landing and in the gym or wherever, these people would cry in secret.

That was part of the scene. Inside, everybody was afraid to be in there. And they'd cry. They just wanted to act hard until the cell doors shut. That's the way I felt because I was like that too. I acted all hard when the doors were open but when the doors were closed, I was like a little mouse, praying for somebody to come and help me. When I was behind the prison cell doors, I realised where I was headed. I had a good look at myself, 'What am I really doing with my life? Where's my life going? Why am I like this?' All these questions were going around in my head and I didn't know what to think or feel.

* * * * *

You might think that my health improved the

second time I was sent to Mountjoy Prison. It did at first but it didn't last long. As soon as I got used to prison life, I found out how you could get heroin. And that second time in prison, I did.

It was easy to get heroin in the 'Joy. You could get everything you needed to take drugs in there. At the time, I didn't even know how it was smuggled into the prison, where they got the needles from, or where they got tin foil from.

That was the little prison secret. The 'Joy was full of little secrets. For tin foil, we would order loads of Kit Kats. Anything that had tin foil on it would do. The prison guards wouldn't give tin foil to inmates, and they wouldn't let addicts near the kitchen area. But no one thought it was suspicious when we bought loads of Kit Kats.

It was easy to get the works in Mountjoy; that's needles. There were lots of needles in the prison; in fact there was everything you needed to take heroin. You just had to know how and where to get them.

Heroin itself was freely available. Even though the guards knew who the druggies were, they couldn't stop us. They searched us after every visit but they still couldn't stop the flow of drugs.

The prisoners devised loads of ways to smuggle drugs. Sometimes they'd use kids, handing them over the counter with the drugs hidden somewhere on their clothes, or they'd kiss it across.

Because it was freely available, I started to get back into heroin in a big way, and by the time I got out, I was worse than when I went in. To this day, I don't know how I didn't end up being infected with HIV. I was so bad that I remember taking a used needle straight from someone else and shooting up with it. I knew these particular girls had HIV but I was so desperate to get high that I didn't care. One girl shot up first and then passed the needle to the other. I could hardly wait for my turn. Once she had her turn-on I just grabbed the needle from her. I didn't even clean it; I just squirted the blood out of it and shot up immediately.

I have since been tested for HIV several times, and thank God, I've escaped the virus. I really don't know how. I was extremely lucky.

* * * * *

On the outside, Ma and Da were devastated. They kept on asking themselves how it had come to this. Even though Ma had shoplifted and been in jail, there were never drugs in the family.

Da's family had never been involved in drugs or with the police. There was a real stigma with having their daughter on drugs. They were excluded from society and made to feel as if there was something wrong with them.

People in the community were talking about me all the time.

'What's wrong with Julie; is she on drugs?' They whispered behind Ma's back, and stopped the conversation when she walked into the shops. Everybody knew. It was like my parents were scarred or marked.

'Oh don't mix with them O'Tooles, Julie's a drug addict and she robs.'

I was a big embarrassment for my parents, and it made their own lives harder.

At the time, I was so wrapped up in myself and my own problems that I didn't even think about them. I was crying every night but my parents must have been going through hell.

* * * * *

When I got out of Mountjoy I went straight back into what I did before. I got so used to the lifestyle that it was easier that way. I knew where to go and who to go to. I knew that if I didn't get money in town somewhere I could always rob something from my family and sell it.

But something had changed. I'd think to myself, 'What am I doing? This is awful.' I wasn't getting any pleasure from heroin any more. The thrill and the buzz that it gave me at the start was now gone. Once I took heroin to make me feel good. Now I took it to feel normal. If I didn't take it, I felt physically sick. I took heroin in the way that many people take coffee first thing in the morning.

But that changed with time. Now it wasn't filling a need anymore, and I found myself feeling empty again. I used to go to the church in Marlborough Street and just sit there and think, 'God, my life is awful.'

I was very unhappy and I was desperate. I was searching for something, but I still didn't know what I was looking for. I was watching my life going down the drain and I wanted the answers to help me, but I didn't know which questions to ask.

I sat in the church and I talked to myself, but I knew I was talking to God. Instinctively I knew He was the only person who could see my heart now, and see what I wanted from life.

I was never really a religious person, but I always believed there was a God up there. Like a lot of drug addicts, I felt that every time I did something wrong, God was marking it down.

Every time I robbed something I'd be looking up to Heaven, waiting to be struck down. I knew I was doing wrong. Little did I know that God was going to bring people into my life who were going to help me.

He knew I didn't want to be the way I was. Deep down, I didn't either, cos it wasn't really me. The deeper I got involved in crime, and the more shoplifting and drug running I did, the more I thought, 'I really shouldn't be doing this.'

I started going to the church cos I'd reached a new low. I'd been thrown out of home. Ma was so tired of dealing with my tantrums, my mood swings and my blatant drug taking that she decided the only way to handle me was with tough love.

I was completely out of it at home one day and she asked me if I was going to clean myself up.

'I'm grand, Ma. There's nothing wrong with me.'

'Well, if you don't want to change, I can't make you change, but I'm not supporting your drug habit any longer,' she said.

She told me to get out and I wasn't allowed home until I cleaned myself up. This completely shocked me and I didn't know what to do. I went to a hostel for homeless people called Regina Chambers on Stanhope Street on the north side of Dublin.

The place was run by nuns and was a type of last chance saloon for people who had nowhere to go. It was set up for homeless people, but it turned out that a lot of drug addicts started going there too, so when I was thrown out, I went to them for help.

Most of the time, I would just sit around their day room, wondering what to do with myself. They didn't have a bed for me initially, so I ended up sleeping on benches in Fairview Park. I stopped washing; I stopped eating. I stopped caring about anything. Drugs were truly dominating my life at this point and they were the only thing I thought about during my waking hours — how I could get drugs, where I'd get money for my next fix, where was I going to get my next high.

Eventually they offered me a bed at Regina Chambers and they asked me to come in. I knew it was a holy place, cos I'd seen the religious pictures all over the walls and the windows, but this didn't comfort me. It didn't intimidate me either, however. I knew from other people, and from my own limited dealings with the nuns that they were kind and honest people.

Even though I was delighted to get off the streets, I'd be lying in bed in Regina Chambers, looking at the cross on the wall, I couldn't stop asking myself, 'What am I doing here?'

'Am I going to be like this for the rest of my life?'

The answer was always, 'Yeah, you're going to be like that, if you want to be like that.'

It was during this period of my life that I realised, for the first time, that if I wanted to change my situation and my life, I had to take control of it. I often thought about how my mother felt. She would ask me how I could hurt her so much. Before she threw me out,

I remember telling her, 'Ma, I want to change. I just don't know how to. I long to change. I don't want to take drugs.

'There's just something in the air. It's like a different person running my life for me.'

It was completely down to my Ma that I turned my life around. If she hadn't thrown me out that time, then I would have continued just as I was. I had to get really low, before I could start to come up again.

I knew it was down to me. The problem as, I just didn't know how to help myself yet.

Sometimes I'd think about ending my life because I didn't want to be the way I was. I didn't even know how I had got so deep into addiction and crime. I just got entangled so fast. I went from drinking to smoking hash, to being a chronic heroin addict.

I thought about dying a lot. I knew drugs were not good for you. That much was obvious. Every day you heard of somebody overdosing, or somebody dying, or somebody in hospital. The fella I was with at the time overdosed so many times that I lost track.

I gradually came to conclude that there's no way a person can deal with that. You just can't survive like that. You either die or you change. I realised that I couldn't carry on with my life as if everything was all right.

I missed being a teenager. I used to sit and think of all the times I played football and won trophies. When I was 13 or 14, I did well for myself. And then I just changed so dramatically. When I thought about these things, I would walk along with my head down, because I'd be thinking, 'Look at the people I've hurt and look what I'm doing to my family.'

I was stuck in a rut. Heroin had me by the throat. It was like there were demons or devils or something, forcing me down a road I didn't want to go.

This might sound crazy but I began to question everything that I was doing. And for the first time, I began to say I would try to stop doing all the bad things that I had done in my life.

It started with shoplifting. I remember saying to myself, 'okay, I'm not going to shoplift, because if I don't shoplift then I won't be able to get any drugs. I'll just give them up.'

I have to admit that this idea didn't work very well. I'd go off robbing a few hours later, and then I'd start thinking in my head, 'I told myself I wasn't going to rob today.'

I was always so disappointed with myself when this would happen. But I eventually learned from this. I knew there was another force behind what I was doing. It was the heroin. It had such a hold on me; I couldn't control it. If I had known at the start what heroin would do to me, I wouldn't have taken it. I never saw the bad side of it back then. I hadn't seen the desperation that it caused in people. I'd just seen the nice picture, getting stoned and having a good time out partying.

At the time, I didn't believe anything that people told me. I hadn't wanted to see the way heroin left people; not a pick on them, no teeth, in bits dying, sick, degrading yourself, doing things with your body that you'd never normally do.

I started to realise that people had tried to warn me, but I didn't listen to them. I started thinking, had I missed my chance? And I didn't think heroin was going to let me give it up.

CHAPTER 9

AT SAME TIME that I started wanting to get off heroin, I met some people from an organisation called Victory Outreach. They were a group of people who were trying to help heroin addicts get off drugs.

I used to see them hanging around outside clinics. They often went up to people and said they'd send them to England where they could get off heroin for good. They said they had a mission there and sent people over all the time, because they knew Ireland was full of drug addicts, and somebody needed to help them. I didn't really know much else about them. But I later found out they were an international organisation with centres in the UK and America.

The first people I met from Victory Outreach were an English bloke called Steve and an American girl called Crystal. They tried talking to me as I was going into the clinic.

Steve was tall and skinny, and you could see by the structure of his face that he was a reformed drug addict, but he was now just your typical bloke. That was the thing about them. They were ordinary people, but they were all former drug addicts. They told me how they'd been junkies for years, but had managed to get off it. They said it was always possible. Steve used to tell me, 'Julie, you know, you don't have to live like this.'

At night going to sleep I would be thinking of his words. Deep down I didn't want to be the way I was. It's just that I was caught up in it and I didn't know how to get out. I didn't know how to ask for help. I was afraid I was going to die if I stopped taking my maintenance, because that's what people were telling me.

I guess you could say that with patience and time, the people from Victory Outreach slowly began to wear me down. A friend of mine, Smally, convinced me to go along to their premises on Talbot Street. I started going to their meetings. We'd just sit around and swap stories, eating biscuits and drinking tea. I never took much notice of what they were saying.

Although part of me wanted to get off heroin, the rest of me couldn't accept that I wanted to. I know that sounds strange, but I guess anyone with an addiction will understand.

My addiction was really bad at this stage, probably the worst it ever had been. I wasn't looking after myself at all, and it was during this period that I was sleeping rough in Fairview Park that I started meeting them.

Smally came to a few meetings but soon stopped. He didn't make it in the end, and he's another friend that I watched being buried. I've always felt terrible that I'm still here and he's not. I'm grateful to him for bringing me to those first few meetings.

Steve often saw me strung out, and sometimes he'd wait outside the clinic for me. The porter in the clinic would say, 'Oh yer man's outside there waiting for you.'

'He's not waiting on me. He's not me friend,' I'd reply, horrified that the people from the clinic would think I was hanging around with Victory Outreach.

But he *was* waiting for me. I think he actually asked what times I went in and out of there because it seemed to me every time I walked out he was there with other people, and they'd say the same thing, 'Julie, you don't have to live like this. There are better things in life.'

'God doesn't want you like this. God didn't make you to be like this.'

'Yeah, yeah, whatever, whatever,' I replied again and again.

Even though I thought God was up there, I thought he'd more likely want to punish me. I'd ask myself, 'Why would God want me to be saved?'

I shrugged it off as if I wasn't listening. They didn't know that when I was going home that night I'd be in bed in Regina Chambers, lying there, and I'd be crying because I'd realised the same thing. I didn't want to be the way I was. I just couldn't help it. I didn't feel strong enough to get out and I couldn't see a way.

Steve never gave up though. He kept following me and saying these things to me. One thing that did make me stop and think about what he was saying was that I'd seen my friend from Sheriff Street go from being a junkie to what she is now — a beautiful woman.

She'd come off heroin, she looked great, and here she was now trying to get others to do the same. They slowly started making me realise that I needed help, that I was a drug addict and my life was going nowhere.

When they would tell me, 'I used to be a drug addict,' they got to me and I would think, 'Wow, I want to be like that.'

I just wanted to be normal again, to wake up and not need a fix. There was a time when I used to go to places with Ma, like Bettystown or Mosney, and we'd stay over. Now I couldn't do anything. I couldn't go away overnight because I had to go to the clinic every morning. They wouldn't trust me with a 'takeaway' cos I'd always messed up in the past. I had given dirty urine — urine with heroin in it, so this made it impossible to go anywhere or do anything.

I'd end up sitting around wishing I was the old Julie, the one I used to be. It made me angry and I wouldn't be able to talk to anyone without swearing at them or calling them names. I was so unhappy with myself, and I was so full of anger and bitterness. But then there was Steve. Whenever I met him, he kept telling me that I could be normal again, if I really wanted to be. I just didn't realise how true this was.

One thing Steve did make me realise was that I had to accept what my life had come to. This was what I had been handed, and he said that I had to accept it. I had accepted that I was going to be a drug addict all my life. It was when I started to realise that this was affecting every part of my life, I began to change. Not only that, I began to ask myself why heroin was controlling me, and why I was missing out on a lot.

I blamed everyone for my addiction. I blamed Ma, Da, God — everybody except myself. Slowly I began to realise that I needed to face up to the fact that I was responsible for my own actions. This was all right if I was talking to Steve or Belinda, or Crystal, cos they'd support me. But if I was talking to Ma about it, even if I said I wanted to get clean, it would end up in a fight. I'd burst out the door, and I wouldn't come back for days. She wasn't trained in dealing with drug addicts and I was still very aggressive and full of rage.

With Steve and Belinda it was good, cos they became my friends before they became anything else. They had more of an impact on my life than anyone at the clinic ever did.

The more my life started going downhill, the more I saw of them. It was as if it was all planned out for me; it was part of my destiny to meet them.

One of the doctors at the clinic used to read from a book, and that really irritated me. I'd be thinking, 'You don't know what I'm going through.' That was the difference with Steve and Belinda — they did know what I was going through, cos they'd been through it too. There was a connection there.

At the same time though, I was really bad, a chronic addict. I was still in bits. I was a disgrace to the family. The cancer drugs were making me hallucinate. I'd see rats on the walls everywhere. I was really paranoid. I just didn't know what I was doing or how I was getting from one place to another.

One minute I'd be walking down the street, then suddenly I'd be swinging out of a car. Next thing, I'd be sitting in Store Street Garda Station, not knowing how or why I was there. I was running amok. I was depressed too, really depressed at what I was doing to myself. But despite really wanting to stop, it took something dramatic to put the wheels in motion.

* * * * *

The only surprising thing about my overdose is that it didn't happen sooner. I had been skirting the edge of life for some time, but had somehow managed not to overdose, despite the amount of drugs I was taking.

It happened on a Friday evening in February 1996. I had just come out of the clinic on Amiens Street and I was sitting outside the Macushla bingo hall nearby with two girls and a bloke, waiting on the fella that I was with at the time to show up.

I didn't know what I was doing and I didn't really care. I was fed up with life and in particular, the way my life was going. I was allowed back on takeaways by this stage, so I had my weekend takeaway from the clinic and loads of tablets. At this time I also had some rohypnol and I didn't know what I was doing with them or what they were for.

I used to buy them from other addicts to get stoned. I would buy them outside the clinic or nearby at the Anna Livia drop-in centre. Then I'd swallow them, simply to lose control of myself. I loved that feeling of floating along, having no sense of what was happening to me or around me.

I didn't intend to OD. That wasn't me. Some people OD on purpose, because they really feel that there is nothing else left for them.

I felt that there was no hope for me, because I was beginning to realise that the more I met the people from Victory Outreach, the more I realised how bad I was. Before I met them, I didn't consider myself a chronic user. I thought I was all right actually. I was hanging around with people just like me, so it made me feel normal.

At that point, though, I thought I may as well die. It wasn't like I planned to kill myself or anything, it was more that I felt there was no point in living.

I drank my whole takeaway for the weekend, and then I took whatever tablets I had on me, along with three rohypnol. I was already spaced out before taking these, and then I passed out.

There were a few people with me at the time, but when somebody ODs, you don't want to get the blame, so they must have legged it and just left me there on my own. Luckily for me, my sister Olivia found me at the stairs of the bingo hall and brought me home. At this stage we were living in Oriel Street cos the Irish Financial Services Centre had bought our old area.

Olivia thought I was just stoned and so never said anything to Ma, because she didn't want Ma to see me like that. Her knowledge of drugs was so little that she didn't know I had overdosed. I couldn't even walk so she carried me all the way home. If she hadn't found me I'd probably have been found dead at the steps there.

Olivia brought me upstairs into the box room in Ma's. She never said a word cos she was afraid. Olivia had never touched drugs in her life. All she ever wanted to be was a professional footballer, and she's always been fit and healthy. She never even hung around with people who took drugs, so she had never seen the affect it could have on people.

She left me there and never said anything to Ma because she thought I'd just wake up later with a bad headache. She didn't know what else to do. How could she know? Ma came up later on and I was black and blue and in a coma. I was unconscious.

An ambulance came and took me to the hospital. I remember when I was in the hospital I could hear people screaming and I could see Ma and her friend Bernie. She was the one that I asked to have a turn-on with, when I was completely out of it.

I remember seeing her face and Ma's face and they were both screaming hysterically. I was completely hazy and thinking, 'What are they screaming at?'

Obviously I didn't know I was in an overdose situation. I thought I was just lying there, feeling fine, and they were screaming and shouting. It was only days after I came around that Ma told me everything.

'The doctors told us you were dead. That's why we were screaming and shouting.'

I do remember parts of it. I must have been going in and out of consciousness. I wasn't in a ward, I was just lying on a trolley, and I remember them shaking and shaking me. The next thing I knew I started feeling my heart slowing down. I don't know whether this is going to sound weird or not, but I felt as if I took a step back and I was looking at myself lying on the bed. I felt my heart beating slower and slower, and I felt myself trying to reach out.

I was slipping; slipping away into darkness. It was very hard for me to see the lights although I kept trying to hang onto the light, it was getting dimmer and dimmer. I was dying, and my heart was slowing down. I remember a voice saying to me, 'If you don't change, Julie, you're going to die like this.'

The voice was so soft, but at the same time, there was much urgency in it. It was warning me. I got a fright and I didn't want to die. I was trying to grab hold of something. Most people are afraid of dying, but to die of drugs is another thing altogether. I could feel evil grabbing me and trying to pull me down. I knew I was going to hell and I was so frightened, so I fought hard to keep hold of the light.

I believe that the voice was God telling me that if I didn't change I would die. There was nothing unusual about the voice. It was very ordinary; no big boom or shining lights, but I believe it was God nevertheless.

I believe in God and I believe that God makes divine things happen. This was divine intervention. My friends had left me to die, because nobody wants to get blamed for anybody overdosing. If my sister hadn't walked by there I wouldn't be sitting here writing this book. But she did. There is a reason for everything.

Then all of a sudden, I just snapped out of it. When I woke up, the doctors were all around me and I was just like, 'What's going on? Where am I?'

I had survived but I was lucky. They put me into a ward and they pumped my stomach. I had taken too much methadone, along with mixing it with the other drugs I had taken. That wasn't my intention. I didn't think I would even have enough in a bottle to kill myself — that's how bad I was. I remember being in the hospital and just waking up and when I really came around I realised what had happened. Ma, Da, Bernie and Olivia were just sitting there.

'How did I get here?' I asked.

I panicked immediately and jumped up out of bed. I asked the doctor if I could go home.

'No, we have to keep you under watch for three days.'

That whole thing happened on the Friday and I was in hospital till the following Monday. It felt as if someone else had now taken control of my life. I was being carried along by another force. When I woke up, heroin had lost its deathly grip. There was only one place I could go now.

* * * * *

When I got out of the hospital, I went to Ma's house. On Wednesday morning I collected my labour and went straight down to Victory Outreach in Talbot Street.

I stood in front of Steve and took a deep breath. 'Okay, I want to go now.'

Steve was standing there with Paul and Marie, who ran the place at the time.

'I want to go to the women's rehabilitation home,' I stammered.

They were so kind. They didn't ask what had changed my mind; they didn't seem surprised. They just accepted what I said.

'Okay. Come back later,' Marie said.

I gave them my money and walked away. Within an hour they had a ticket booked for me to go to London that night. I went down and collected my methadone from the clinic and I went that evening.

I stopped off to get some clothes before I left. When I told Ma she thought I was joking. When she realised that I was serious, she was delighted. I hadn't discussed it with anyone. I hadn't even thought about it. When I went home and told her what I was doing, she started bawling crying. She was praying that something like this would happen to me, that I'd get help. I just said to her, 'Ma, I'm going to Victory Outreach.'

She knew that meant going to London, so she asked me how I was going to go and I said, 'I'm after collecting my labour and I gave them the money.'

That was something I'd never normally do. There was no way I would have given away my own money in the past — especially my own labour money. Ma started running around the house, still crying.

'What do you need? What about that?' trying to give me everything she could find. In the end, I just went with a little rucksack. I think there was only a toothbrush and some underwear in it. I didn't see Da that evening as he was working. I wasn't upset or anything. It just happened. I needed to go away as soon as I was ready because if I had time to change my mind I wouldn't have gone. I just knew that if I didn't go, the next time I would take heroin I was going to die. Even today I still carry that in me. That's what keeps me away. I'm afraid that if I take heroin again, I'll die.

Later that night I went to the airport but I didn't go on my own. Ma, Olivia, Anthony and Ryan came to see me off. The Victory Outreach people also came. They had the ticket and were holding on to it. Belinda was already there. She had gone six months previously, and she was coming home frequently.

Belinda and another girl from Pearse Street were going back to London that night, and they'd booked me onto the same flight as them.

My family were all hugging me and kissing me, and I remember I got drunk cos I was afraid of what was waiting for me. I was drinking whisky just to help me get through it. I knew what I was facing. I was coming off 250mls of physeptone, which is a really strong dosage.

It was very emotional at the airport. I could see the hope in my family's eyes and I didn't want to let them down. I knew what this meant to them — it represented a new start for us as a family. Ma looked hopeful for the first time in years.

But I went missing for about half-an-hour. I knew this was a turning point but I was still weak. I had a bit of hash and I smoked it. I knew I had to do this, cos I just wanted a bit of time to myself. At the same time I knew that with the lifestyle I had been living, I was never going to be able to go back to doing anything like this. This was the end of it. So I went off on my own, I had a few joints, and I took a few tablets.

I thought that if I got loads of drugs into me at the beginning, then I'd be okay for a few days. I was emotional. I was terrified. I knew I had to do it, but I needed a crutch to help me take the first step. When I went missing Ma nearly lost her mind. She thought that I had backed out, and she nearly hugged me to death when she saw me walking back to them.

Drug addiction is hard to beat. Even when I was taking those last few tablets, I knew that I had to stop. All I could think about was the hospital. I couldn't stop thinking about my out of body experience and I knew I wasn't going anywhere but down. I knew then that I had to grab control and to fight my way back up in life. With this knowledge, I went back to my family and knew what I had to do.

When I stepped on to the plane, I had taken drugs for the last time. I thought my life was well over. I was only 21 and I had already been dragged to the ground. It's sad to think that at 21 years of age I was the way I was. I was so mature, so grown up and streetwise in ways when I shouldn't have been.

I went through so much when I shouldn't have gone through any of it. But I knew the day I overdosed, it made me come to my senses. I needed it to happen. I needed something drastic to change me. The clinics couldn't change me. I was just a number to them and I always felt like I wasn't anything important. It felt like nobody cared the way Victory Outreach cared.

Standing at the airport, all I could think about was, out of all the people in Sheriff Street, why had this happened to me. Out of all the young ones I took drugs with, why did I live when they died?

That was the turning point in my life. I didn't know at the time. And it was planned — not by me. I just turned up.

Saying goodbye was awful. As I got on the plane, I actually thought I was going to lose the plot. I wanted to believe that I was going to start some type of new methadone programme, or whatever, although I knew that wasn't how Victory Outreach worked. I brought a big bottle of methadone with me, just to have, but I was in for a shock.

* * * * *

We landed in Stanstead an hour later. By this time, I was out of it, because as well as all the tablets, I had taken loads of physeptone. I was still thinking in my head, I'll just do this one more time because I know when I get off this plane I'm never ever going to take drugs again.

I was afraid. I was so terrified. I'd never taken this type of step before. I'd never been so far away from the world I knew. I'd been to France that time, but there was a gang of us then and I knew what to expect. Now, I was lost.

Sheriff Street was my world. I had never seen anything beyond my own streets. I didn't think there was a world beyond Sheriff Street. I remember getting off the plane and thinking, 'Am I doing the right thing here?'

I was afraid that I might fail, or that something bad was going to happen, because in my head I was thinking about a counsellor who'd said to me, 'You're on too much phy. You're going to die. You can't come off that amount. It's too much.'

At the same time though, I knew I had to do this. In the depths of my heart, I knew I had to do it, because if I didn't, I was going to die. It was that simple. Knowing this didn't make it any easier, though.

At Stanstead, Belinda informed me, 'There's no drugs and there's no smoking and you can't write to anybody.'

And I started thinking, 'Oh God. Help me through this.'

I started wandering around the airport, waiting for a chance to take my tablets and drink the phy, and Belinda started chasing me and shouting, 'Where is she? Where is she?'

I just thought I'll get wrecked one more time, even though I knew in my heart I had to get clean.

'I'll take all these and it will block out what I'm afraid of, because I'm afraid of doing it.'

I remember Belinda chasing me around the airport, trying to get my bag of drugs. Thankfully she eventually caught me. When I walked downstairs, they let me have one last smoke. Ma had bought 60 Benson and Hedges, so I said, 'Just let me have one more smoke, just one more smoke.'

If I'd known I couldn't smoke or drink or do anything like that I probably wouldn't have gone, so it was a good idea that they left it till I got off the plane in London to tell me.

When we collected our bags, we went to a women's place where I was told I was going to get clean. I think the place was near the Whipcross Hostel in London; it was called South Woodford. It was an old English house that lay off the beaten track. There was a park and a lake there. The house was huge, with about four bedrooms. A couple called Debbie and Dave Gibbs ran the place. They weren't drug addicts but they ran this centre with

Victory Outreach for people trying to kick their addictions.

There was an Irish girl there called Sharon, an English girl called Mandy and then there was me, Belinda and the girl from Pearse Street. There were one or two other girls but I don't remember their names.

They searched all my stuff like they would do in any rehab. Then they sat me down and introduced me to everybody. They showed me around the place, the bedrooms, the grounds and they told me the rules.

'This is what you can do, this is what you can't do,' and all that. There was more about I couldn't do than what I could do. That was hard but I don't think it was any worse than anywhere else. Every place has their rules. Even at home they all had their rules. After they made me a cup of tea they brought me upstairs. Belinda gave me fresh clothes and I had a shower, and then she told me that she was going to help me. She said she was going to be with me through my withdrawal sickness, because she knew it was going to be hard on me. It helped me and I believed her because she was a former drug addict herself.

It's strange the things you remember at times like that. I remember the stairs were skinny and everything was brown. The carpet was dark brown, the walls were light brown, and it was all wallpapered. There was no paint. I remember thinking that was a bit odd. This was going through my head and there I was being told how I was going to be cured.

My room had a set of bunk beds on one side and another set of bunk beds behind the door. I was given a bunk bed behind the door, on the bottom. For four days, that's where I stayed cos I was just out of it. All the drugs I had taken before I left Dublin were still in my system. I was really bad at that stage. Methadone gets into your bones and takes all the marrow and all the goodness out of you. It had left me destroyed.

I didn't look good physically. I was six and a half stone and there wasn't a pick of meat on me. I was just a bag of bones. I remember lying on the bed thinking, 'If I don't stop feeling the way I'm feeling, I'm going to disintegrate.' I was touching my legs and hips and thinking, 'Oh God. I'm wasting away.'

For the first time I really had a good look at myself, and I thought, 'There's nothing there.'

Then it really started hitting me. You see, as a drug addict the heroin gives you a false idea of yourself, a certain confidence, and you're looking at yourself and you think, 'Oh, I'm all right. I'm not that bad.'

When I hadn't had heroin for a couple of days, I actually thought I was going to get crippled or something like that. My bones and all my joints started to hurt really badly — ankles, knees, the back of my knees, elbows, neck, hips and my teeth.

One of the major problems I had to contend with was that I wasn't only addicted to heroin, and every drug I could get my hands on, I was also addicted to methadone from the clinic. Heroin just withers away your flesh. But methadone is harder to come off than heroin. The chemicals really get into you and strip away your whole body. That's why so many people lose their teeth. Most ex-addicts have a weird kind of a look about them, their faces become sunken.

It eats away from the inside. I realised that's what had happened to me. I had lost my body.

I cried for two weeks, and it actually brought me back to reality.

The people at Victory Outreach told me I wouldn't get anything to help me through the withdrawal. I thought I was hearing things. They said they were going to give me God and pray for me. I threw a tantrum and went ballistic.

'I need methadone and you're going to give me *God*?'

Even after my experience at the hospital when I overdosed, I still thought, 'Oh my God, what am I after doing?'

I didn't realise they were so religious. I wasn't sure what was going on and I was getting nervous. I started having second thoughts. As soon as I heard the word 'God' and that they were going to pray for me, I freaked out. I was expecting a rehab course, or maintenance or something like that, and instead I was getting God and prayers.

Belinda, who was my assigned counsellor, said they didn't believe in giving me methadone to come down off heroin, and they didn't believe in giving me sleeping tablets to come down off methadone, because they would simply be taking away one addiction and giving me another.

'You don't understand. I'm doing 250mls of physeptone. My doctor said I needed it.'

Belinda stood her ground and just told me that I wasn't going to get anything. Dave, who ran the financial side of things, simply laughed at me.

The other girl who was going through the same thing with me said, 'These are religious freaks. They're going to do something to us and they're going to cut us up or do something and make us do mad things.'

The first thing I thought of when they said they would pray for me was, 'Hare Krishnas!'

'Oh my God, I'm going to get me hair shaved or something,' I said to the other girl, 'Do you know anything about these people?'

'No, they just told me that they were going to help me.'

But she wasn't as bad as me. I think she was just a problem child, because she was very big but she wasn't scruffy or down and out. She came with a big haversack. I just came with a little bag with underwear in it and a toothbrush and toothpaste.

For the first four days I was okay, then the real withdrawal began.

CHAPTER 10

WHEN THE WITHDRAWAL started in earnest, I felt as if my body was falling apart. The pain was unbearable. My skin crawled. It felt like rats were eating me alive. I got sick and my head pounded. I'd never felt so sick in my life. It felt like the bed was sucking me up, because I was lying there and all I could feel was pain . . . pain all over me. They gave me painkillers but nothing stronger, and nothing was able to quell the agony. Instead of giving me what I wanted, they gave me what I needed.

They gave me baths and prayed for my soul. Belinda sat up with me morning, noon and night, putting Deep Heat on me and rubbing stuff on my legs, because I actually couldn't physically lift my legs off the bed.

I was in a state. My body collapsed. I'd been running around doing all kinds of things for eight years, never stopping to think about the damage I was doing to myself.

During those eight years that I took drugs, I had stopped looking after myself. I was doing all kinds of things that wrecked my body. Looking back on what I'd been doing, and seeing what it did to my body, now made my skin crawl.

It was only during my recovery that I realised how sick I had been. Nature had been trying to shut my body down, trying to protect it. While I was on physeptone and heroin, I stopped menstruating for three years. My body held a lot in. About three months after I stopped taking drugs, my body started to function again and my cycle slowly returned to normal. Apparently this is quite common. Some women's cycles don't return for years after they get off heroin.

The withdrawal was so bad I wanted to die. I was in bits and I couldn't do anything. It was like everything caught up on me at once — emotionally, mentally and psychologically. I started to think about things I never thought about before, and then I started to think of the hurt and the pain I caused Ma.

In some ways I knew I had to go through the pain. I was aware that I was coming back to reality. I thought about my teenage years. I asked myself, 'What happened to me?' I could have been something.

I was a great footballer, just like Olivia, but I always thought, 'Why was I never like my sister? Why did I never make it up there?'

It would have been a dream come true to play football for Ireland with my sister. It might not have happened, it was just a dream. But at the same time, in my wildest nightmares, I never thought I would end up the way I was, lying in pain in that bed.

I didn't eat. I was capable of getting into the shower but I wouldn't wash myself. I would just sit there and the water would just come down on me. Belinda would just stand there for a while and then say, 'When you're ready just call us, or we'll just collect you in 10 or 15 minutes.'

I went through this, probably for about three or four weeks. I didn't eat properly for months. I had a bowl of cornflakes and that would be it. My stomach wouldn't be able to take that much. It was folding up. My ribs stuck out and my bones protruded. I was emaciated. I carried no weight and I couldn't eat. I looked like death warmed up.

The counsellors prayed for me during all of this. They all came in and said, 'We're going to pray for you. You know, Julie, God never intended for you to be a drug addict. He gave you life to enjoy, not to destroy.'

The more I was there, the more they seemed to make sense to me. They'd say, 'God made you. He created you. And He didn't create you to destroy yourself.'

At first I would say, 'Yeah, go on.'

And then they'd say to me, 'You're trapped. You were trapped by heroin.

'How many times did you tell us that you really wanted to be off this, that you really wanted to get better today and then you found yourself in town robbing or getting stoned again?'

'Yeah, that's true,' I'd admit to them. They knew about addiction. They knew about the need. They knew what it was like for a junkie. You have to get heroin. Your body tells you, 'I need heroin, I need heroin, I can't do anything without heroin.'

It suddenly all started to make sense. As I got cleaned up, my senses came back to me. I knew that they were telling the truth. They'd say, 'You don't deserve to be like this. You deserve better. I used to be a drug addict. I used to be the way you are now.'

Now, coming off the drugs, seeing for the first time what the drugs had done to me, opened my eyes to the way my life really was.

The pain was a journey of self-discovery. Another thing that I learned was that I had stopped growing emotionally. I'd cried in prison cos I was afraid, but the last time I cried out of sadness was when I was a kid. In the area I lived, I felt it was always a case of, 'be hard, don't let anybody see that you're a bit of a crybaby. They'll make a laugh of you.'

If you cried, you wouldn't be in the gang, or you wouldn't fit in because you were a wimp. Behind closed doors in prison I could let it out. The more the heroin left my system, the more I cried.

I hated myself for what I'd put my family through, for what I'd put my parents through. I found it hard to accept what I'd done. Then I thought about my brothers and sisters and the trouble that I'd caused them.

I used to start fights the whole time. I'd start them without any provocation. I'd just be sitting there and I'd throw something at someone or I'd give them a slap on the back of the head for no reason.

I was just mad and angry because I was a drug addict. I couldn't comprehend what I had done. The names I called people, the way I behaved towards certain people, it was because I was angry. I was especially sad at the way I brought shame to Ma and Da though, because they brought us up really well and taught us to always respect our elders and never give cheek back to anybody.

They told me I used to be like that, a respectful person, but that it totally went out the window when I went on drugs. I was so ashamed.

There were times though when I wanted to leave South Woodford to get drugs. I still felt I needed drugs. There were loads of times I said I wanted to leave, to give up. But they wouldn't let me. They didn't want me to fail.

The counsellors were very experienced and would just say, 'Come on, Julie. It's only for a couple of days that you're going to be like this. Come on, you're nearly there. You're five days or six days away.'

We were allowed watch television, but I wouldn't have the mind to. I'd be just decked out, lying there in agony. I haven't experienced that kind of pain since.

I thought my body was disintegrating. The more I lay in bed the more it hurt me. I knew I had to go through this. It was something that I couldn't avoid.

Because I had taken so much physeptone, it was extra hard on me. Since then, I've seen girls come in and come off heroin and it was nothing for them compared to what I went through.

The time came when I just couldn't look at myself anymore. The first time I examined myself soberly, I got sick. I was disgusting and horrible. I was just bones. You would think I had malnutrition or something, or that I hadn't eaten in years. It looked as though I was trying to starve myself deliberately, like I had some sort of disease or something.

I wasn't a pretty sight, but I needed to look at myself, because I needed to see me for who I really was, and my life for what it was.

The truth was that I didn't realise how bad it was going to get before that day came. I thought it was all good for me at the start. It always is with heroin. I was all happy and everybody was doing it, but then when I was strung out I was left on my own, and nobody wanted me — only my family.

After two weeks in detox they let me contact home, so I wrote to Ma. Belinda had told her I'd arrived safely two weeks previously and that I was getting through it. It was hard writing to her. There was a distance between us.

They never locked the door, so I thought about getting out, but Belinda always told me, 'Julie, no, you're not going anywhere. You're staying here.'

And I'd be like, 'Please, Belinda, please.' She'd be firm, but kind as well, 'You're going to be all right in a couple of days. You're going to be all right.'

I was still rolling around in the bed in pain a lot. My body was detoxing itself. I had constant diarrhoea and I was vomiting frequently. I had experienced nothing like it.

As the days went on it got better and the pain started to ease. Every day I felt a little bit better. Better in my body, and in my mind. The counsellors never stopped talking to me. They'd talk about when they were on drugs and what people did to them. They spoke about how people treated drug addicts — because they came across some people, wicked people that did horrible things to addicts.

I used to see the dealers come into Sheriff Street from other areas. They wouldn't touch drugs themselves, but they used to shout, 'dirty addicts' at us. We were good enough to sell drugs to but that was all.

I talked with Belinda for hours about certain things that had happened to me. When she would reply, 'Oh that happened to me as well,' it made me feel like I wasn't alone.

Emotionally I fell apart and I had to put myself back together again. One thing you have to do though, to be able to get better, is to forgive yourself. They told me that if I didn't forgive myself it would drive me back, back to drugs.

From the age I started taking drugs, being the 'psycho' that I was, it was very hard to show emotions, when I wasn't crying. You think you can bottle it all up and then it goes away. But what you're actually doing is suppressing it by keeping it down, until eventually it boils over. For me it came out in a flood. I was crying for weeks in there. I'd stop for a while, and then something would remind me of certain people or my family, and I'd just start bawling all over again. They explained to me why this would happen — all the people that did bad things to me and all the bad things I did to other people was coming out of me. Healing my emotional scars took a lot longer than getting over my physical addiction.

I didn't look any different, but I felt different. When I looked in the mirror it was still me, but inside I was better than before. I felt loved, I felt wanted. The people from Victory Outreach lived by the bible and they said it was God's love they were showing me. So I always felt like I was loved. It was funny because I felt like I got more love and attention from them than I did from my own family. When Ma threw me out, I thought that she didn't want me any more, but I was wrong. She just didn't know how to handle me.

The first time I spoke to her from England, I spent the entire conversation just crying. I remember her saying, 'I love you. I'm glad you're there. Please stay there. Your Da's all right, and Anthony's all right.'

She started going through the whole family. 'Gary's all right, Lindsay's all right and they all love you and they miss you.' All I could say was, 'Yeah that's good.'

Though I wanted to go home, I kept telling her that I wanted to stay. Deep down I wanted to do it. I am where I am today because I was willing to change. The counsellors would not have been able to help me if I wasn't willing to let them. If they'd told me to stand on my head for ten days and then get down and shake, do a Hare Krishna dance and things like that, I would still have done it. Because I was desperate. I would have done anything. I had done mad things for drugs, so why should I not do them to get off drugs?

That was how they got through to me in South Woodford. They would say to me, 'Come on, you were mad when you were on drugs. How come you're not mad to do it now?' That was their way. They knew how to get into a drug addict's head. They knew how I thought about things.

It took me a long time to get my head around it. To this day I'm very forgetful. I'd forget what I was doing last week. If somebody said, 'The other day when I was talking to you, do you remember I told you . . .'

I'd have to say, 'Hang on for a minute.' We'd be sitting there for a few minutes and I'd say, 'Oh yeah, I remember now.'

I'd have to go back. It wouldn't just come to me. I'd have to go back a few memories. There are some things in the women's home in England that I have just forgotten, I don't remember parts of it now. I remember getting off the plane, but I don't remember getting on it. I remember the airport. Maybe I just didn't want to remember the plane journey because I was in such fear of what was waiting for me on the other side, I was determined not to go back.

* * * * *

I spent five months in London. After I'd recovered enough to leave my bed and was able to be trusted walking around, I helped out wherever I could. The people at Victory Outreach in South Woodford used to do church functions, and we would go sometimes to clean people's houses, do little jobs and stuff like that. They would help us with understanding ourselves and personal development. It wasn't like we would all have to sit down and have a chat. It would be more like, if you were in the house and a conversation came up, then that was that. That was their idea of personal development. But they also taught me how to pray and how to read the bible. I had never been very interested in that. At first, I was nervous. 'You want me to read the bible? I'm not reading that.'

I used to think the bible was the little book that I got on my communion day. I was afraid to go near it. I knew I was in sin; I was the biggest sinner going. I was into drugs and robbing everything that wasn't nailed down. I used to think, 'I'm not touching that book.' I thought that if I touched it, it would strike me down.

I later found out that these people were Born Again Christians. Before I knew what religion they were, I used to think, 'Is this a cult or what? What are they going to do with me?'

When my mother heard that I was reading the bible, she was concerned. She was a Catholic, and she didn't know who I was with. The bottom line was though, she didn't care what they did, as long as they got me off drugs. And she always says, it was divine intervention by God that they were sent. Because it was weird they were just right smack bang in the middle of Sheriff Street, and we lived there. It was like they were sent to us, particularly to my family.

Ma would say, 'They're okay. They just help people to get off drugs.'

They used to tell me about God, and I really thought they were trying to entice me into something. You have to admit when a lot of people hear about God a lot they think, 'Are these religious freaks? What are they? Monks or nuns?'

But as time passed, it all made sense to me. I came to believe that I was trying to fill a void in my life with drugs, men, money, everything. And no matter what I did, I couldn't fill it. It was only when I found God, that I realised none of these things would ever fill the void.

* * * * *

I don't feel the need to take drugs anymore. But I still have the spiritual belief I gained when I was with the Victory Outreach people in England. Now I spend all my free time in Victory Outreach. When I'm not at home, that's where I can be found. I'm just helping out and trying to pay them back. I owe my life to them and God. I really do. What if they never came to me? Where would I be?

I'd only be a picture on a headstone somewhere in a graveyard. I'd be just another dead drug addict. Just another statistic. I strongly believe that.

I was born a Catholic so I thought, 'Is this right? Am I supposed to be doing this?' I was with Victory Outreach for so long I just got used to it and then I really started believing it. When I started seeing other drug addicts arrive and overcome their addictions I thought, 'This is real.'

I believed it in my head, but not in my heart. There were times I'd think, 'I'm just going to leave them now. I got what I wanted. I'll see you later. Thanks, but I'll see you later.' But the message got through to me. I started believing in God and that He can change a person.

I don't need drugs now. The emptiness is filled. I don't have to pretend to be someone else, I can just be myself. I have that confidence now.

I'm not going to be something that I'm not. I was always trying to be somebody that I wasn't, to fit in with everybody else. That made me put all my efforts into drug taking, going out dancing and being with everybody; and all the stuff that comes along with that.

After a few months of being off drugs, I became more content with my life.

They taught me about God, about loving myself and having self-confidence, taking care of and respecting myself.

It took about three months for my body to recover properly and to be free of heroin and methadone. It was a painful recovery but a positive one nonetheless.

CHAPTER 11

ALTHOUGH I WAS clean, I was still mentally craving heroin. I had come to hate the drug, but I was still at risk. Heroin addiction never leaves you. It lingers in your memory — always waiting.

I didn't return to Ireland when I got clean because I felt I might start using again. Instead I stayed in London helping other addicts. It was my way of paying back Victory Outreach.

However, after five months, the people in Victory Outreach in England sat down with me and told me that the place was closing down. They asked me what I wanted to do. The first thing I told them was that I definitely didn't want to go back to Ireland. I had strong urges to use heroin again. I said that if they sent me back to Ireland I would end up back on drugs. I was all right physically but mentally I still wanted it, the addiction hadn't been broken just yet.

I really wanted to make it, in my heart. It was a big step for me to go to Victory Outreach in the first place, to admit I was a druggie and that I needed help. Having gone through the pain of withdrawal and dealing with my past, I refused to risk losing it all.

Victory Outreach have pastors who are similar to reverends, and one of the pastor's wives suggested I go to Victory Outreach in California, where I could go to the women's rehabilitation home and hopefully completely break the need for heroin. I jumped at the chance. I needed to get a passport first, so I came home. I wanted to stay well away from Sheriff Street, so I stayed with a couple in Blanchardstown.

Ma paid for my plane ticket to the States, even after all the stuff I did to her. That meant a lot to me. I said goodbye to my family, knowing I wouldn't see them for a while. It was hard, but I knew that if I didn't do this, I was most likely going to end up back on heroin, and it would kill me in the end.

Victory Outreach in California was in a place called San Bernardino, in the middle of nowhere. It was a real shock to the system. I have really pale skin and I found it hard to get used to the heat over there. My face was permanently red from the sun and the heat. It was a culture shock too. There were 32 girls there and the place was so big, you could get lost in it. It was very hard to get used to, but it was the best decision I ever made. It worked for me and it's working for other people still.

It really was like nothing I'd ever seen before. There were so many different cultures and races living side by side. They ate differently, they spoke differently — everything about them was different. I had no experience in dealing with other cultures at all and I got lost for a while. I was hiding there, and going through the motions.

I realised that I would have to go back home some day and I still had things inside myself that I needed to deal with. There were so many insecurities, past hurts and low self-esteem issues I needed to address. Most drug addicts will agree with me when I say that there is usually something deeper behind their addiction.

Nobody wants to stick a needle in their arm every day unless they are ill. Loads of people had tried to change me over the years. They tried to change the way I looked, the way I acted, all the stuff on the outside, when what was really wrong was on the inside.

Drugs was the wall of defence that protected me from having to talk to anyone. I was the youngest of the older set of kids growing up, so I was always told what to do. I hated that, and when I got older I didn't let anybody tell me what to do. That got me in trouble a lot. I had a problem with authority — with the police, my parents, school — and this messed me up.

I thought it was me against the world. I had to deal with the way I treated the rest of my family too. I had treated them really badly. I was like an animal, filled with rage and I had to come to terms with that.

At Victory Outreach they dealt with all of these things. People would open up and start talking about past hurts and experiences, and it all came out that way. It was like personal development. I was only starting to learn things that I missed out on when I was a teenager. I learned how to be affectionate towards people.

I also learned why I went wrong and why I was there, and why God wanted me to be better. My eyes opened to what was around me. As time went on I was getting better and better and it became more and more of a life-changing experience for me rather than an automatic way of responding. It was all coming out as little things, sometimes good and sometimes bad.

Once we were all getting into a van to go to a job. We had jobs to earn money to keep the rehabilitation homes opened, because they don't receive government funding. One girl was a couple of minutes late and so we all got punished for her actions, where we had to get up early and do really bad cleaning chores.

I went ballistic and dived on her, swinging punches at her. Luckily I didn't hurt her, but that was the old me, wanting to kill her and call her all these names. It revealed my heart to everybody. They were all going, 'Uh oh, Julie's not fixed yet. Another few months for her.'

After that, I realised I'd have to really try to change. Otherwise, I'd go back to the life I left behind. Maybe not straight away, but I would eventually. And that would mean I was going to die from drugs.

I know that it was only God who helped me through that period. It was so hard for me. I didn't know anyone over there and I still had that 'them against me' attitude. I felt alone and I couldn't associate with them.

However, I worked really hard, looked deep into myself, and came to terms with all of my problems. In the end, I came through it.

In February 1997, Eleanor Garcia, the home director told me I would be graduating in a few weeks and I would be going back to Ireland. She had been so kind and welcoming towards me, but I told her that I wasn't ready yet; that I still had a number of issues that I needed to work through.

'Your testimony is no good here. You need to show other addicts in Ireland how it has worked for you. No one in America knew you when you were addicted,' she reminded me.

I knew she was right. My demons were all in Ireland — my old friends, family and Sheriff Street. I had to go home to face those demons.

I graduated on 1 March 1997. I was so nervous about going home. I left America on

16 March and I landed in Dublin on Debbie's birthday, Saint Patrick's Day.

I completed a second phase when I got home, where they taught me how to get back into society, become a better person and how to get a job. Victory Outreach had also trained me as a counsellor, so I could help other people addicted to drugs to fight their addiction.

They had opened a women's home in Leixlip and a girl called Marcella ran it. I completed my second phase there and then got a job in the amenities centre in Leixlip, which I loved. The people were so nice. When I came back from America I had to start all over again.

I had to make new friends, see new places and new environments. It was like starting secondary school again. I had to change the way I talked, so I didn't sound like a drug addict, and I didn't walk like one anymore. I had a new heart. That was what I needed; not a new body or head. Just a new heart.

Life got so much better. I finished a football course. To settle back in, I also got a cleaning job and got my driving licence. I knew I had boundaries. There were certain places that I couldn't go, certain people that I couldn't hang around with, and certain things I couldn't do.

I can now walk through Sheriff Street and if I see a drug addict I'll say hello — I'd never just walk by — but I can't get back into their lifestyle. I do what Steve and Belinda did for me. I try to help them. I try to give back to other people because my life was saved.

When I came back to Ireland, I spent most of my time with Victory Outreach until it was time for me to stand on my own two feet. This was something I had never done.

After a year I went to the job centre on Amiens Street to look for a job. I found a job on the internet there, in a bank, so I applied straight away. I never thought I'd get it. I got an interview, went along, and a couple of hours later I got a phonecall saying I'd got the job. I couldn't believe it.

I worked there for four years. My life has changed so much, and I know I shouldn't even be sitting here now. I know I should be dead. There are plenty of other people out there who never made it. I have buried a lot of friends. That's why I am so grateful now, and I spend every free minute I have with Victory Outreach, trying to give back what they gave to me.

I want to help as much as I can, cos I am so grateful for my second chance. I'm grateful to God, and to everyone who showed me support, love and care. There were so many things I never noticed in the world, but now I notice and I appreciate everything — the trees, the sun, even the rain — whereas before I took it for granted.

I'm now married to Gerard, who I met at Victory Outreach. We got married in July 2005. My life has changed so much.

I have travelled a long road. I have my own flat, my own car, and a job in the bank. When I was on drugs I wanted to rob the bank! It's amazing what's happened. Sometimes I have to sit down and think about it all. It's still fresh in my mind. As long as I remember, I'll never go back to where I was. I know it could easily have been someone else who was saved, and I could be the one lying in a grave.

You might think that I never think of heroin anymore but the truth is that I never stop thinking about it.

A few years after I left Victory Outreach, I remember writing to my parents to say that I was sorry for all the things I'd done. It took a long time for me to forgive myself because I knew the hurt I had inflicted. When I came home Ma didn't really trust me straight away, so I knew she was still hurt. I had to earn that trust back. Now, we're great friends, thank God.

I'm glad that my father lived to see me come off drugs. I think I was six years clean when he died. I do forgive myself but sometimes I think back in horror and regret. Certain things remind me of stuff that I did to my parents. In my head, I say that I'm sorry. I don't say it to Ma but she understands; she knows.

She's delighted with me now. She can't believe that I got married — she's just blown away by it. She's shocked, because she probably thought in her head, 'Julie's going to die like that. She's going to die a drug addict.' And you know, there's an old saying, 'Once a drug addict, always a drug addict.'

People think like that, saying, 'She's never going to change.' And a lot of people did tell me, 'You're never going to change. You're always going to be like that. You're never going to survive.' Even before I went into Victory Outreach, the fella that I was with said, 'There's not a hope for you. You're never going to come off all that phy. How are you going to do that?'

And I was telling him, 'I'm just going to do it. I don't care how I'm going to do it. I just need to do it. And I need to do it now.' And I said to him, 'You go to the men's division and I'll go to the women's' but he wouldn't.

I sometimes meet people who knew me when I was using drugs. When I came back from America, I went to see my old counsellor at the clinic and she was just shocked. She was shocked and delighted for me.

The fact that I am here today, telling my story, shows that we can overcome anything. When I look back over it all, at everything that happened and everything I thought and felt, from my childhood in Sheriff Street to where I am today, I realise how much I have grown. I was lost before, and I had no idea of my place in the world. I didn't know where to fit in — with my family, with my friends, even with other drug addicts — and I felt a big empty hole inside myself.

Now, that hole is no longer there. God has filled it for me, and it was always Him who could fill it. I just didn't know before.

· I wrote this book because I wanted people to see there is always hope. No matter how dark the tunnel is, there is always light at the end.

All my life I tried to be somebody I wasn't. I tried to be what everyone else wanted me to be. I never felt like I fitted in or was accepted in society. I thought I had to be a certain way, or hang around with certain people to be accepted. That was one of the reasons I turned to drugs.

Today I don't need to be somebody I'm not. I'm who I was always meant to be and I'm doing what I was meant to do; helping people who are like I once was. I love my life now and I wouldn't change it for anything in the world. When I was a drug addict, I had no life.

I hope this book will encourage people to change. If my story gives just one person enough strength to walk away from drugs, and to take their life back, then it will have been worth it.

Don't think that just because you're not from Sheriff Street that you are safe from heroin. Heroin use has traditionally been confined to Dublin, but this is no longer the case. In the past few years treatment clinics have been established to deal with heroin use in Galway, Waterford, Athlone, Portlaoise, Carlow, Tullamore, Drogheda and many other towns.

You mightn't be aware of it, but it's never far from your doorstep. For me it started with hash and progressed from there, so don't stand too proud when you put this book down. The next time you see a heroin addict, remember how easily it can happen, and how, it often isn't their choice.

They are somebody's daughter, sister or mother. They are somebody's son, brother or father. They are just like me. They are just like you.

EPILOGUE

My life since the publication of Heroin
February 2008

WHEN I FINISHED writing *Heroin* in 2005, I felt like I'd undergone the world's most effective therapy session. It was like my life was a jigsaw puzzle and every chapter of the book helped me to see the overall picture more clearly. I had initially hoped the book would help other addicts out there, but it is only now that I realise how much it actually helped me. It forced me to revisit a lot of painful memories, and at first I found this hard. I even felt angry — over the fact that several years of my life had been lost to drugs. While other girls my age were worrying about their hair and make-up, I was too busy worrying about my next fix to care about my appearance. When I was on heroin, the days, weeks and months all blended into one. My addiction caused me to miss out on so much and I worried that this was all down to karma — that just as I had robbed from people in the past so I could buy drugs, heroin had robbed from me in turn by taking away a big chunk of my youth. But since finishing this book, I've realised that as crazy as it sounds, if I could go back I wouldn't do anything differently. All the terrible things that happened were part of my destiny because if I hadn't gone through them then I wouldn't be able to help other addicts today. By making peace with my past, I was then able to think more clearly about my future.

The first decision I made was to quit my bank job and start working full time for Victory Outreach. It was one of the best decisions I've ever made. My husband and I are now in charge of the women's rehabilitation centre in north Dublin. Women of all ages pass through our doors — from teenagers to middle-aged women. And although they all have different

stories, they usually overlap on one point —
they all have low self-confidence and don't
love themselves enough. They think that
by taking drugs they'll be more likeable and
better able to fit into the world. The first piece
of advice I give them though is that if you can't
love yourself then you'll never be able to love
anyone else. And that's the problem, heroin
becomes the only relationship addicts are
capable of holding down. They'll lie, steal and
cheat on everyone else in their life, but they'll
do absolutely anything for heroin.

We usually have an average of eight women
staying with us in the centre at any given time.
By now, word of mouth brings a lot of these
women to us, but sometimes my husband and
I will go out on a Friday night and approach
girls working on the streets. They're usually
wary of us at first, and I can't blame them — I
was exactly the same when Steve and Crystal
first tried to explain Victory Outreach's Bible-
based treatment programme to me. When
you've lost all faith and hope in everything, it's
hard to believe that God could possibly still
have some faith invested in you.

Not all of the women in the centre manage
to stay clean though — some are back using

after a few days, some last a few weeks, and others manage to stay clean for several months. It's hard to see them come so far, only to fall at the final hurdle. But as hard as it is to break the physical dependency on drugs, it's even harder to break the emotional ties. Some girls just aren't ready to make the leap of faith, and others may get there eventually, but they're going to take the long way around. I compare these girls to the Israelites in the Bible. They spent 40 years wandering around in the wilderness before finally reaching the Promised Land, when if they had just stayed with God and entrusted themselves to him, the journey would have taken them only 14 days.

A lot of girls come to the centre because their parents have begged them to, but they have no real intention of getting clean. I think you have to live your own life though and make your own decisions — and your own mistakes too. Until you consciously decide that you want to come off drugs, people can try and change you all they want, but like a spring, as soon as they loosen their grip on you you're going to bounce back into your original shape.

We don't offer methadone in the centre; we're one of the few rehabilitation centres in

Ireland who believe that going cold turkey is the best option, even if it's initially the hardest one. But if you give someone methadone to come down off heroin, then what do you give them to come down off methadone? It doesn't make sense — especially when methadone is known to be even more addictive than heroin. I remember being told by doctors in the past that my body had been pumped with too many drugs to be able to cope with going cold turkey, so for a long time I never thought I would be completely free of drugs. The methadone clinics didn't work for me and I was attending them for years. They focus on the physical side of the problem, and neglect the emotional side. They offer you counselling if you want it, but even though the doctors and psychologists have plenty of degrees and masters between them, their only knowledge of drug addiction is gained from reading about it in books — they don't really know what you're going through. They have never experienced the panic and horror that sets in when you need another fix but don't know where you're going to get the money to pay for it. And they haven't ever felt the agony of withdrawal symptoms when your body is crying out for more drugs. The great thing about Victory Outreach is that all of the people who work there are ex-addicts who have gone through it and somehow managed to come out the other end. And now I'm one of those people — after years of being called a 'dirty junkie', people now look up to me. I've had some addicts come into the centre who knew me when I was still using, and they say, 'If Julie O'Toole can do it, and we all know what Julie was like, then so can I'. I came from nothing, and now I have everything. I feel like I could keep giving and giving to the girls in the centre for the rest of my life, and yet I will still have more than enough left for myself.

I have witnessed success stories amongst my family and friends too. My sister Debbie, who was getting clean just as I finished this book in 2005, has been off drugs for three years now and is living a very happy life in America. And my friend Belinda, who accompanied me over to England when I first started the Victory Outreach programme, is also still clean. She recently enrolled as a student in Trinity College. So there is life after drugs, and my biggest challenge is convincing the addicts I meet that they too can get clean and make something of their lives.

Eighteen months ago my dream of having my own family came true with the birth of my son. The explosion of happiness I felt when the nurse placed him in my arms was overwhelming. The chemically induced highs I experienced on drugs can never compare to the natural highs that you experience as a mother. He looks just like his dad but he has the O'Toole smile. While he's still a baby, I feel like I can protect him, but I know that he'll eventually come into contact with drugs. My plan is that when he's old enough to understand, I will educate him as much as I can on the dangers of taking drugs. I won't just point at pictures in textbooks and wag my finger at him; I'm going to show him pictures of both his father and me when we were at our worst, all skinny and yellow in the face, with our eyes glazed over and our teeth rotting in our heads. I don't want him to memorise the different nicknames of drugs, or their effects; I want him to witness the cold-hard reality of it, in bold colour, so that he knows just how ugly drugs can be.

Even though cocaine is a less addictive drug than heroin and causes fewer deaths each year, it gets far more attention from the government and the media — most likely because it is a middle-class drug. Heroin is associated more with the working-class, and just as in the 1980s the government tried to brush the problem under the carpet, they are still doing the very same thing today. Even worse, methadone clinics are offered up as the solution — the government seems to think it deserves a pat on the back for weaning addicts off heroin by transferring them over to methadone. But the best way to help addicts is by getting them off drugs altogether. I also think that all this talk about legalising drugs is ridiculous — it may help to reduce the profits of criminals, but I think if drugs are more freely available then you're going to have more young people experimenting and getting hooked on them.

The best way to reduce drug usage is by providing non-sugar-coated education in schools from people who've gone through addiction. When my book was first released in 2005, I started getting calls from local schools asking me to come in and talk to their students. The children were so curious and were very open and honest, asking me questions such as, 'How did you start taking drugs?' or, 'How good do they make you feel?'

I remembered back to when I was 13, watching the older kids taking drugs and not knowing what they were doing or what the risks were; all I knew was that they were laughing a lot, and looked very happy as a result. If I had known then that the laughter eventually gives way to so much pain, I wouldn't have been half as curious.

There is one question that has arisen several times during visits to schools, and one which I can never answer: 'Well my Da (or Ma, sister, brother...) is on drugs, so how come you came off them, but they can't?'

As hard as it is to communicate the dangers of drugs to kids, it's almost impossible to explain heroin addiction to anyone who hasn't experienced it for themselves. It's like heroin becomes so much a part of you that breaking free of the addiction is a little like being handed a chainsaw and being asked to sever your own limb.

It's been 12 years since I last took drugs and I have no desire to go back to that life. In the past, I saw heroin as a way of escaping from my insecurities and I thought that the more drugs I took the more distance I could put between me and my problems. I thought I was shooting up to get high when really all I was trying to do was make myself numb to the painful low my life had slumped into. I didn't believe the world had any happiness to offer me and I didn't think myself worthy of any kind of happiness anyway. I now know differently. Today my life is filled with the kind of happiness that doesn't ring hollow. It is rooted in God, my husband, and my son, and all the love and affection I get from them and that I give in return.

The heroin epidemic has spread outside of Dublin so there is an increasing need for rehab centres across the country. In July of this year Victory Outreach plan to open a centre in Belfast and my husband and I have been called on to run it. I am excited about making the move and the change of scenery but most importantly I'm happy to be able to continue reaching out to other addicts through my work with Victory Outreach. I feel eternally grateful to God for giving me this second chance in life and I want to repay him by dedicating my life to helping other drug addicts overcome their addiction.

If you or your family have been affected in any way by the issues raised in this book, you can contact any of the following institutions on a confidential basis:

Victory Outreach Dublin
vodublin@hotmail.com
Ph: +353 (0)1 8349580

The Drug Treatment Centre Board
www.addictionireland.com
info@dctb.ie
Ph: +353 (0)1 6488600

The Hanly Centre
info@thehanlycentre.com
Ph: +353 (0)1 2809795

The Samaritans
jo@samaritans.org
Ph: +353 (0)1850 609090

Merchants Quay Ireland
info@mqi.ie
Ph: +353 (0)1 6790044

MORE NON FICTION BY MAVERICK HOUSE

THE MIRACLE OF FATIMA MANSIONS
An Escape From Drug Addiction

By Shay Byrne

The *Miracle of Fatima Mansions* is the moving story of a teenage boy who lost himself to drug addiction after the death of his father.

Set against the backdrop of working-class Dublin in the 1970s, Shay Byrne has written a brutally honest account of his addiction, his crimes and his redemption.

Byrne narrowly escaped death during a violent attack at Fatima Mansions, the flat complex synonymous with extreme social depravation, social decay and drugs. It was the unlikely location of an epiphany that would transform his life.

The incident forced Byrne to confront his inner demons and seek help at a radical treatment centre.

Told with searing honesty, Byrne's debut book is the most insightful, candid and thought-provoking book ever written on Dublin's drug culture. It is destined to become a classic.

MORE NON FICTION BY MAVERICK HOUSE

HELL IN BARBADOS

BY TERRY DONALDSON

Hell in Barbados is the powerful true story of a drug-addicted smuggler who found his salvation in the unlikeliest of places. Told with disarming honesty, the book propels the reader into the mind of an addict and shows us the depths of degradation one man sunk to before finding the inner strength to save himself. Terry Donaldson met with success early in life but his struggle with addiction soon became an all-out war. His Jekyll and Hyde lifestyle – TV presenter by day, whilst he scoured the streets of London in search of drugs and prostitutes by night – caused him to lose everything.

Facing financial ruin, he agreed to smuggle drugs from Barbados, but was caught and sent to one of the world's worst prisons, where he remained for over 3 years. Honest and disturbing, *Hell in Barbados* is the true story of how Donaldson witnessed stabbings, beatings, shootings and a full scale riot as the prison went up in flames. In this extraordinary book, he describes the true horror of prison life in the Caribbean, the depravity that brought him there, and the years of brutality he was forced to endure.

To order this book, go to www.maverickhouse.com

MORE NON FICTION BY MAVERICK HOUSE

THE A TO Z OF IRISH CRIME.
A Guide to Criminal Slang

This book is a highly entertaining introduction to the world of criminal slang.

Those who are hell bent on breaking the law have created their own unauthorized and underground language that is often more colourful and vulgar than plain English.
If you are interested in speaking the language of the street, or want to converse with fences, street walkers and the army, this book is for you.

Forget what you learned in English class, this book is the definitive guide to the ever changing language of the street.

To order this book, go to www.maverickhouse.com

MORE NON FICTION BY MAVERICK HOUSE

MISS BANGKOK

Memoirs of a Thai Prostitute

By Bua Boonmee

Miss Bangkok is a vivid, powerful and moving memoir of a life spent in prostitution in Thailand. Poor and uneducated, Bua Boonmee escaped an abusive marriage only to end up in the go-go bars of Patpong. There, in the notorious red-light district of Bangkok, she succumbed to prostitution in an effort to support her family.

Bua's story is one of resilience and courage in the face of abuse and poverty. Her confessions will make you laugh and cry, cringe and applaud. She will change your perception of prostitution forever.

To order this book, go to www.maverickhouse.com

MORE NON FICTION BY MAVERICK HOUSE

THE SUSPECT

The Story of Rachel O'Reilly's murder

By Jenny Friel

On a clear autumn morning in 2004 Rachel O'Reilly, a 30 year-old mother-of-two, was brutally battered to death in her home. It was a merciless killing that stunned the small, trusting community where she lived, and devastated her close-knit family. In the days that followed the discovery of her body, it was thought that Rachel was the victim of a bungled robbery attempt. It soon emerged, however, that police investigating the case believed Rachel had known her killer and that her murder had been carefully planned months in advance.

The spotlight immediately fell upon Rachel's husband, Joe O'Reilly, who admitted in a number of extraordinary press interviews that he was a prime suspect in his wife's slaying. The 32-year-old advertising executive vehemently denied any involvement. It was a crime that captured the imagination of the public, who watched as the illusion of the idyllic suburban life the couple shared together began to shatter.

To order this book, go to www.maverickhouse.com

MORE NON FICTION BY MAVERICK HOUSE

WELCOME TO HELL

One Man's fight for Life inside the Bangkok Hilton

BY COLIN MARTIN

Written from his cell and smuggled out page by page, Colin Martin's autobiography chronicles an innocent man's struggle to survive inside one of the world's most dangerous prisons. After being swindled out of a fortune, Colin was let down by the hopelessly corrupt Thai police. Forced to rely upon his own resources, he tracked down the man who conned him and, drawn into a fight, he accidentally killed that man's bodyguard. Colin was arrested, denied a fair trial, convicted of murder and thrown into prison, where he remained for 8 years. Honest and often disturbing, but told with a surprising humour, *Welcome to Hell* is the remarkable story of how Colin was denied justice again and again.

MORE NON FICTION BY MAVERICK HOUSE

THE TORSO IN THE CANAL

The Inside Story on Ireland's most Grotesque Killing

By John Mooney

John Mooney's controversial new book explores the horrific killing and dismemberment of Kenyan immigrant Farah Swaleh Noor by Dublin sisters Linda and Charlotte Mulhall, dubbed the 'Scissor Sisters' by the media.

Noor's dismembered body was cut into pieces before being dumped in the Royal Canal in refuse sacks.

The Torso in the Canal explores the circumstances surrounding the notorious killing, and the effect it had on those involved. Based on exclusive interviews with relatives, friends and investigators, this comprehensive book reveals new information about the investigation and the backgrounds of both the killers, and their victim.

MORE NON FICTION BY MAVERICK HOUSE

BLOOD AND MONEY

By Dave Copeland

Filled with paranoid mobsters, clever scams, and deep betrayals, *Blood and Money* gives a unique insight into one of the most successful gangs ever to operate on American soil.

By the time Ron Gonen arrived in New York City he had broken out of prison in Germany, been exiled from Israel, fled England as a prime suspect in a multi-million dollar crime ring, and had been chased out of Guatemala.

Gonen lived life in the fast lane until things spiralled out of control.

In the 1980s, a small group of Israeli nationals set up one of the most lucrative crime syndicates in New York City's history. With rackets ranging from drug dealing to contract killings, their crime spree was so violent that it wasn't long before they were dubbed the 'Israeli Mafia'.

The gang went to war with the Italian mafia, killed Russian gangsters and pulled off the biggest gold heist in the history of Manhattan's Diamond District.

They would have become the most powerful gang in the New York underworld had Gonen not decided to risk his life and become an FBI informant. *Blood and Money* is his story.

'*A thrilling guts-and-glory look inside the Israeli organised crime machine of 1980s New York City.*' - *Publishers Weekly*